AF654128

The Modern Ayurvedic Cookbook

A contemporary approach to an ancient tradition

The Author

AMRITA SONDHI is a certified yoga instructor, Ayurvedic cooking teacher, and owner of Movement (movementglobal.com), a cutting-edge clothing line specializing in sustainable fibers; she also was a co-founder of lululemon athletica, the activewear company. She lives at Bowen Island, British Columbia, Canada.

An all-vegetarian cookbook based on
Ayurvedic principles

The Modern Ayurvedic Cookbook

A contemporary approach to
an ancient tradition

Amrita Sondhi

Orient Publishing
DELHI | MUMBAI

Dedication

I dedicate this book to all my invaluable comrades, students, and teachers, the 'fringe dwellers' who keep pushing the edge on the 'new normal' by practicing and regenerating the ancient healing arts; to those who pursue and create breakthroughs in health by being shining, living examples of vitality; and to the community of yogis and yoginis — locally and globally — who keep connecting to the source and transmitting the light.

ISBN : 978-81-222-0533-6

The Modern Ayurvedic Cookbook

Subject: Cookery / Health & Healing

© 2006 Amrita Sondhi

1st Published 2013
6th Printing 2024

Published in arrangement with
Arsenal Pulp Press, Canada

Published by
Orient Publishing
(an imprint of Orient Paperbacks)
5A/8 Ansari Road, New Delhi-110 002)
www.orientpublishing.com

Printed and bound at TACT Printers, New Delhi

Contents

Acknowledgments

I would like to thank my parents, family (all of you!), and friends who have always stood by me as I have gone off the beaten path. Joan and Nevenka, thanks for being shining examples of practicing what you preach, and having fun while doing it! Sandra Sammartino, thanks for synthesizing all your yoga knowledge, for being an invaluable teacher who appeared at the perfect time in my life, and for showing me how to transmit from my spirit, connect to the source, reconnect to my body, and how to pass on that learning. I would like to thank all who have hosted or helped me with cooking classes and fundraisers for the Pamoja Foundation. And to the residents of Bowen Island, among others, who constantly encouraged me to write this book and share my knowledge of Ayurveda, and who helped test recipes. Finally, I would like to express my deep gratitude for the wonderful team at the publishing house who worked tirelessly to help make this book a reality.

Introduction

Ayurveda: The Tradition of Healing

ORIGINATING IN INDIA MORE than 5,000 years ago, Ayurveda is the oldest system of healing. The name derives from two root words in Sanskrit (the ancient Indian language): *Ayus*, which means life, and *Veda*, which means knowledge or science; therefore in English, Ayurveda is 'life knowledge' or 'life science.'

At the heart of Ayurveda is our intimate connection to the elements in nature, and how they can help us to achieve a physical and spiritual balance in all aspects of our lives. For the sake of our health and well-being, this balance can be accomplished through a number of means, including diet and exercise.

The ancient sages of India, believed that all material forms, including our bodies, are made up of five essential elements — ether, air, fire, water, and earth — in varying degrees, maintaining a balance among these five elements is key to our physical, mental, and spiritual health.

Historically, the ideas and philosophies of Ayurveda were transmitted orally through the Vedas. The oldest of the Vedas is the 'Rig Veda' ('in praise of knowledge'), which is almost as old as Ayurveda itself, and describes healing herbs and how they can be used. Later, by about 500 BCE, Ayurvedic knowledge began to be written down by the writers Charaka, Sushruta, and Vagbhata, which hastened its popularity. It continued to thrive under Buddhism and the rule of

Ashoka the Great, and spread to China and Japan. But the Muslim invasion of India in the 12th century CE led to Ayurveda being widely replaced by the Muslim system of healing, then further suppressed centuries later by the British, who wanted to promote the western system of medicine. With the return of Indian independence and the leadership of Mahatma Gandhi Ayurvedic schools and medical practices finally rose once again.

Today, this ancient and holistic healing science is arguably more popular than ever, and is a source of influence for many medical practitioners in both east and west. Ayurvedic schools throughout India teach herbal medicine, massage, surgery, psychiatry, obstetrics, gynecology, astronomy, the use of mantra, meditation, and yoga — among many other healing practices — to improve every aspect of life, balancing body, mind, and spirit.

And most importantly, because Ayurveda considers food an integral part of its healing system, it originated some of the oldest and most time-tested principles of nutrition. Indian cooking uses very many Ayurvedic principles in meal preparation both to maintain health and to cure a variety of illnesses, from the common cold to more serious ailments, with appropriate foods that balance the *doshas*.

These ancient remedies are now being proven scientifically and practiced around the world, most notably by Dr Deepak Chopra, the medical doctor and well-known scholar of Ayurveda.

My journey to Ayurveda started during my mid-thirties, when I burnt out long before most people do. I was designing my clothing line in Europe, manufacturing it in Asia, and wholesaling it across Canada, as well as opening my own retail clothing store in Vancouver. I was on an emotional roller coaster driven by my passions and deadlines — I thought that taking breaks for exercise and making time to cook were self-indulgent — and inevitably, my health began to suffer. Luckily,

I met a private trainer, Joan — now a good friend — and began my slow journey back to health. According to Joan's brochure, 'A man spends his health to get his wealth and then he spends his wealth to get his health back again.' This idea hit home for me. Exercise and healthy eating became an essential part of my daily life. Over time, I became aware of the effects of different activities and nutrients on my body. I started to track my changes according to the various seasons and times of day as well as what I was doing, and what I ate. I learned later that there was a science to it all: Ayurveda.

After my clothing store was robbed, I began practicing yoga to deal with stress, including the breathing exercises (pranayama); this transformed my life. Soon I trained to be a yoga teacher myself, and now have been teaching yoga for over ten years. Yoga continues to have a deep impact on me, showing me that life can be an endless adventure. People who have not seen me for a while are amazed at my transformation, saying I have never looked better. More importantly, I feel better, both inside and out.

Embracing yoga naturally led me to study the Ayurvedic principles of cooking and nutrition. At the same time, this took me back to my Indian roots. Both my maternal and paternal grandparents emigrated from India. I grew up eating delicious Indian cuisine at home, where food was always celebrated. My mother was a great cook.

Through my growing interest in health, fitness, and yoga, I met a great group of like-minded people who were energetic, fun-loving, and interested in improving themselves. We ate together regularly and talked about the latest trends in health, fitness, and diet. We discussed the positive effects of 'super foods' and omega oils; debated over healthy carbohydrates, water consumption, cleanses, and sugars; and shared ideas about macrobiotic and raw food diets, and how to maintain a healthy digestive system.

I learned that to be fit and healthy, one has to cook regularly at home, in order to have more control over what goes into our bodies.

Soon cooking became a new hobby for me. Because of this, searching for the finest and freshest (not necessarily the most expensive) ingredients has become one of my favourite activities; it allows me to indulge in daily treks to the local markets, in search of the most pleasing textures, colours, aromas, and flavours for my dishes.

Since knowing your own personal constitution, or *dosha*, is essential for knowing how to keep your life and health balanced, *The Modern Ayurvedic Cookbook* begins with an explanation of what *doshas* are, and a questionnaire so that readers can determine their own primary *dosha*.

A section on the Six Essential Tastes of Ayurveda follows, which explains how food, specifically taste, affects people's personal constitutions. I then provide basic tips for herbs and spices, and staple recipes for *ghee*, *paneer*, sprouting, and cooking beans, lentils and rice which are traditional to Ayurvedic cooking.

150 easy-to-follow vegetarian recipes make up the major portion of this book. Each recipe has symbols to indicate how it affects your *dosha* (page 34). They also include variations for different *doshas*. Most recipes use whole grains and fresh foods rather than processed foods, which are considered toxic, or *tamasic*, in Ayurveda. Ayurveda stresses eating fresh foods, so I do not emphasize frozen, canned, or microwavable foods.

There also is an extensive appendix at the back of the book to introduce you to eating differently according to each season, and a simple twelve-day cleanse to help clear the digestive tract of toxins and improve the absorption rate of the nutrients you consume. And, since living an Ayurvedic lifestyle isn't just about the food, I also have included a section of yoga postures for your *dosha*, as well as alternative therapies (colour and aromatherapy, and breathing and visualization techniques) that will help you to maintain a balanced sense of being in all regards.

Once you have learned the principles of Ayurvedic cooking, you will know how to balance out your unique constitution with food. For example, you will learn how to use spices to either increase your element of fire (Pitta), or decrease it; how to 'ground' your element of air (Vata) by using good oils or fats and sweet tastes (which are not necessarily 'sugary'; foods such as bread, rice, and coriander are considered sweet in Ayurveda); and how to activate a lethargic state (Kapha) through increased movement and the consumption of more raw foods. Throughout, I explain the basics of cooking and how to get started if you have never tried it before. As a result, you will increase your repertoire of tasty, nutritious vegetarian cooking, and at the same time notice an increase in your sense of balance, well being, and energy.

Some of the ingredients used in these recipes may sound exotic, but most can be found at your local grocery store. These stores usually carry fresh produce, herbs and spices, whole grains, and a wide variety of beans and lentils.

Understanding *Doshas*: Your Body Constitution

WE ARE ALL BORN with three *doshas* (personal constitution) that make up our body constitution. Most of us have a stronger primary *dosha*, a secondary *dosha*, and a third less prominent *dosha*; a few people are naturally balanced in all three.

Ⓥ	Ⓟ	Ⓚ
Vata = Air	Pitta = Fire	Kapha = Earth

It is through Ayurveda that we try to bring all three *doshas* into balance. For example, a woman who is a Vata (meaning her primary *dosha* is Vata) would look to eat foods and engage in activities that are considered to have Kapha and Pitta qualities to bring herself into balance. Since our *doshas* reflect the elements of air, fire, and earth, it is not surprising that our food and environs affect each of these elements differently. For example, some people enjoy spicy food, while others cannot handle it; similarly, some may thrive in cool weather, and others may detest it. On page 17 there is the Dosha Questionnaire, which will help you to determine your primary and secondary *dosha*; you will then learn how to prepare meals appropriate for your body type by incorporating foods or ingredients that reduce your primary *dosha* and increase the other two *doshas*, thus bringing you into balance.

In general, if you feel out of balance, look for recipes that decrease your primary *dosha*. For example, if you are a Pitta, look for recipes that have ' – Ⓟ.' It is important to familiarize yourself with all three *doshas* so you can be more attuned to your body. Don't be afraid to experiment to find out what's right for you!

***Dosha* and Our Lifestyles:** In our modern world, where we are always on the go and cell phones, laptops, and cars seem to be constant companions, it is easy for us to get a Vata imbalance. In general, if our Vata is over-stimulated, we need to calm it by eating warmer, heavier, moist foods with some 'good oils' (page 27), which include the salty, sour, and sweet tastes. Meditation and rest also helps Vata to cool down and unwind. Every time Vata goes into overdrive and we start to feel stressed, it is important to take a silent five-minute break and do nothing.

If Pitta is aggravated, we feel fiery, aggressive, and confrontational. At these times, it is important to eat cooling foods like cucumbers, drink cool (but not cold) drinks, and include lots of raw fruits and vegetables in our meals. Avoid sour, fatty, and spicy foods as well as artificial stimulants. Eat meals in serenity and order, go for walks as much as possible, and avoid strenuous physical exertion or overheating.

When Kapha is out of balance, we feel dull and lifeless, and can't get off the couch. It is important for us to get moving. Regular and varied exercise is extremely important when we have excess Kapha. We also need to reduce butter, oil, and sugar in our diet, increase consumption of foods with the pungent, bitter, and astringent tastes, incorporate stimulating, hot, and spicy ingredients, and avoid cold drinks. To balance Kapha, we should eat light, warm meals, avoid eating to pacify the emotions, and go for brisk walks after eating.

VATA — Element: Air

People born with Vata as their primary *dosha* are energetic, creative, and natural risk-takers who often initiate projects; however, when Vata is out of balance, they experience nervousness, anxiety, fear, fatigue, and depression. Other physical signs of Vata imbalance include constipation, dryness, flatulence, weight fluctuations, poor circulation, decreased sweating, and feeling easily exhausted.

Those with excess Vata or who have Vata as their primary *dosha* should concentrate on calming their anxiety and turning their fear into joy and fatigue into energy by following the Ayurvedic principles.

PITTA — Element: Fire

People born with Pitta as their primary *dosha* are natural leaders and administrators, capable to take precise, decisive, and focused action; however, when Pitta is out of balance, they experience mood fluctuations, irritability, increased body temperature, restlessness, and impatience. Other physical signs of Pitta imbalance include broken capillaries, weight fluctuation, sweatiness, sleeplessness, and an over-active mind.

Those with excess Pitta or who have Pitta as their primary *dosha* should focus on turning irritability into focused, positive action, and balancing body temperature and moods, by Ayurvedic principles.

KAPHA — Element: Earth

People born with Kapha as their primary *dosha* are the pillars of their communities. They have the ability to 'follow-through,' seeing projects to completion, and are affectionate and good-natured, experiencing the least mood fluctuations of the three *doshas*; however, when Kapha is out of balance, they experience sluggishness, feelings of being 'stuck in a rut,' strong attachments, addictions, possessiveness, over-sensitivity, and laziness. Other physical symptoms of Kapha imbalance include excess weight, cellulite, lack of motivation, and puffiness.

Those with excess Kapha or who have Kapha as a primary *dosha* should turn stagnant energy into activity, find freedom from attachments and addictions, and be creators of their own positive choices, by following the Ayurvedic principles for reducing Kapha.

Determine Your *Dosha*: Your Body Constitution

THIS TEST WILL HELP you determine your primary and secondary *doshas*. Take no more than 15 minutes to answer all the questions, as your first response that comes to mind is usually the best one. Circle the number that best pertains to you, and don't worry about being perfect. Once you have answered all questions, add up your Vata, Pitta, Kapha scores separately. The highest number is your primary *dosha*, the second highest will be your secondary *dosha*. Sometimes people have an equal score in all three *doshas*, although this is quite rare. Once you know your primary *dosha*, you will be able to choose foods and activities that keep you in balance and harmony; remember that we each possess a combination of all three *doshas* to varying degrees, and need to keep them all in balance.

It is a good idea to complete this questionnaire twice, the first time informed by your current lifestyle and environment (*Vikruti*) and the second by your experiences as a young child (*Prakruti*). In Ayurveda, knowing the difference between your *Prakruti* and *Vikruti* can give you new insight into your body, and how to restore it to optimal health. An important means of doing this is through diet, but remember that our health is also influenced by our lifestyle choices, environment, emotional state, the amount of exercise we do, and the people around us.

It is also beneficial to do this questionnaire every few years as our body constitution naturally changes over time.

Dosha Questionnaire

Vata	Does not Apply		Sometimes Applies		Often Applies	
I perform activities very fast	1	2	3	4	5	6
I learn quickly and forget easily	1	2	3	4	5	6
I am enthusiastic and lively	1	2	3	4	5	6
I have a thin physique and don't gain weight easily	1	2	3	4	5	6
I am light and fast on my feet	1	2	3	4	5	6
I can be indecisive	1	2	3	4	5	6
I get bloated or constipated easily	1	2	3	4	5	6
My hands and feet tend to be cold	1	2	3	4	5	6
I worry and am anxious a lot	1	2	3	4	5	6
I don't like cold weather, food, or drinks	1	2	3	4	5	6
I speak quickly and my friends consider me a chatterbox	1	2	3	4	5	6
I am moody and emotional	1	2	3	4	5	6
I have difficulty falling asleep or I am a light sleeper	1	2	3	4	5	6
I have dry skin	1	2	3	4	5	6
I have an active imagination and my mind is often restless	1	2	3	4	5	6
My energy levels fluctuate	1	2	3	4	5	6
I get excited easily	1	2	3	4	5	6

Dosha Questionnaire

Pitta	Does Not Apply		Sometimes Applies		Often Applies	
I am efficient	1	2	3	4	5	6
I am precise and orderly	1	2	3	4	5	6
I have a well-balanced body shape and a medium build	1	2	3	4	5	6
I am strong-willed, maybe forceful and am not easily influenced by others	1	2	3	4	5	6
I get tired easily and feel uncomfortable in hot weather	1	2	3	4	5	6
I perspire easily	1	2	3	4	5	6
I am impatient and quick to anger, though I may conceal it	1	2	3	4	5	6
I have a hard time skipping meals	1	2	3	4	5	6
I have a good appetite and can eat large amounts if I want to	1	2	3	4	5	6
I am determined, stubborn, and can be critical	1	2	3	4	5	6
I rarely get constipated	1	2	3	4	5	6
I can be a perfectionist	1	2	3	4	5	6
I prefer cool temperatures to hot	1	2	3	4	5	6
I enjoy cool foods and drinks	1	2	3	4	5	6
Overly spicy foods don't agree with me	1	2	3	4	5	6
I have difficulty with people disagreeing	1	2	3	4	5	6
I love challenges and am focused in my efforts to achieve goals	1	2	3	4	5	6

Dosha Questionnaire

Kapha	Does not Apply		Sometimes Applies		Often Applies	
My actions are slow and deliberate	1	2	3	4	5	6
I gain weight easily and lose it slowly	1	2	3	4	5	6
I am patient and even-tempered	1	2	3	4	5	6
I am not bothered if I skip a meal	1	2	3	4	5	6
I get congested easily and may have sinus problems	1	2	3	4	5	6
I sleep very deeply	1	2	3	4	5	6
I prefer eight or more hours sleep	1	2	3	4	5	6
I am a slow learner but have an excellent long-term memory	1	2	3	4	5	6
I don't get sick often	1	2	3	4	5	6
I don't like humidity or damp weather	1	2	3	4	5	6
I have smooth, soft skin	1	2	3	4	5	6
I have a large, solid body build	1	2	3	4	5	6
I have a slow metabolism	1	2	3	4	5	6
My energy levels are strong and I have good stamina and endurance	1	2	3	4	5	6
I am affectionate, caring, and sweet natured	1	2	3	4	5	6
I eat slowly	1	2	3	4	5	6
I make my decisions methodically	1	2	3	4	5	6

The Six Essential Tastes of Ayurveda

AYURVEDA DIVIDES FOOD INTO six tastes that influence the three *doshas* and thereby influence our overall sense of satiation and well-being. The six tastes are sweet, sour, salty, bitter, pungent, and astringent; each one affects our *doshas* differently. (Many foods have a combination of two or three tastes, such as oranges, which are considered both sweet and sour.) Ayurveda recommends that all six tastes be included in each meal; when they are, we will be left feeling harmonious, peaceful, and calm, as each *dosha* has been nourished. Note that only a little of each taste is necessary for it to satisfy and balance us; more is not necessarily better, and in fact, in certain situations it can be detrimental or toxic.

The guidelines offered here will teach you how to harmonize your *doshas*, and bring yourself back into balance when necessary. Although it is important to have the six tastes at every meal, don't become overly concerned with this, as it should be a goal, not a rule. As you learn to listen to your body, you will start to be attuned to how the various tastes affect you. Remember that as you get to know which tastes are good for your *dosha*, you may not be eating foods you typically would, but it is those familiar foods that may have been sending your *dosha* out of balance. Give your body the time it needs to get used to new tastes, and the subsequent feeling of balance that comes from changing your ingrained eating habits.

Vata is pacified by sweet, sour, and salty tastes.
Pitta is pacified by sweet, bitter, and astringent tastes.
Kapha is pacified by pungent, bitter, and astringent tastes.

Here are the tastes that decrease, or pacify, each *dosha*:

Sweet: Rice, bread, honey, milk, *ghee*, oils, and most 'sweets' are considered sweet in Ayurveda. Most legumes, lentils, and beans are considered sweet as well as astringent, which increases Vata. An exception is urad dal which is considered sweet and not astringent, so it calms Vata. Grains and vegetables, which contain carbohydrates, are considered sweet, and increase Kapha while decreasing Pitta and Vata. Foods with the sweet taste are considered heavy and therefore grounding.

Sour: Lemon, vinegar, yogurt, cheese, tomatoes, grapes, plums, and other sour fruits increase Pitta and Kapha and decrease Vata. These foods should be consumed in small amounts and not at all by those with excess Pitta or Kapha. Sour foods promote digestion, are good for the heart, and warm the body. But an excess of these foods can cause irritation, dizziness, or loss of vitality.

Salty: Salt, soy sauce, pickles and *chutneys* increase Kapha and Pitta and decrease Vata. Having at least a little salt in our diets is essential for our health; it also aids digestion. But consumed in excess, salty foods can cause bloating and water retention, or lead to inflammatory conditions. Too little may result in illness, thyroid problems, or leg cramps.

Pungent: Ginger, cumin, black pepper, cinnamon, cayenne, chilies, radishes, onions, and garlic decrease Kapha and increase Pitta and Vata (but a little of these foods are good for Vata due to their warming effect). Pungent tastes heat the body, stimulate digestion, and eliminate excessive fluids, thereby relieving colds and bronchitis. They also help to get our metabolisms moving if we are feeling sluggish.

Consumed in excess, they can cause anger and aggression, as well as burning sensations, dizziness, dryness, and increased thirst.

Bitter: Green leafy vegetables (e.g., spinach), bitter gourd, turmeric, fenugreek, lemon and orange rind, dark chocolate, and olives increase Vata and decrease Pitta and Kapha. They cool Pitta when out of balance and too fiery, and lighten Kapha when too heavy. Consumed in excess, bitter can produce envy, jealousy, and yes, bitterness.

Astringent: Beans, lentils, apples, pears, cabbage, broccoli, cauliflower, and potatoes increase Vata and decrease Pitta and Kapha. Consumed in excess, they produce flatulence, constipation, and a dryness of the body.

Glossary of Cooking Ingredients

Cereals and Grains

Azuki beans, *Sem*
Barley, *Jau*
Chickpea (Black), *Kala chana*
Chickpea (White), *Kabuli chana*
Cracked wheat, *Dalia*
Gram flour, *Besan*
Kidney beans, *Rajma*
Millet, *Bajra*
Oat flour, *Jaee ka Atta*
Oatmeal, *Jav*
Red beans, *Rajma*
Puffed rice, *Murrmura*
Vermicelli, *Sewain*
Yellow millet, *Peela bajra*

Fruits

Avocado, *Nashpati or Makhanphal*
Blackberries, *Jamun*
Kiwi, *Kiwi*
Nectarines, *Shaftalu*
Peach, *Aarhoo*
Pears, *Nashpati*
Plums, *Alobukhara*
Pomegranate, *Anar*
Raspberries, *Rusbhary*
Strawberry, *Istabary*

Nuts, Oils and Seeds

Almonds, *Badam*
Currants, *Munakka*
Hemp oil, *Bhang ka tel*
Mustard seeds, *Sarson ke daane*
Olives, *Jatoon*
Pecan, *Chhota akhrot*
Pine nuts, *Chilgoza*
Pistachio, *Pista*
Pumpkin seeds, *Kaddu ke beej*
Raisin, *Kishmish*
Sesame Oil, *Til ka tel*
Walnut, *Akhroot*

Spices and Condiments

Asafoetida, *Hing*
Basil, *Tulsi*
Bayleafs, *Tejpatta*
Black pepper, *Kali mirch*
Cardamom, *Elaichi*
Cayenne, *Lal mirch*
Cinnamon, *Dalchini*
Cloves, *Laung*
Cumin, *Zeera*
Fennel seeds, *Saunf*
Fenugreek, *Meethi*
Flax seeds, *Alsi*
Jaggery, *Gur*

Nutmeg, *Jaiphal*
Oregano, *Ajwain*
Poppy seeds, *Khaskhas*
Rhubarb, *Revandchini*
Saffron, *Kesar*
Thyme, *Ajwain*
Turmeric, *Haldi*
Tamarind, *Imli*

Vegetables

Agar agar, *Chini ghaas*
Alfalfa, *Rijak*
Asparagus, *Shatavari or Sootmooli*
Beets, *Chukandar*
Bell pepper, *Simla mirch*
Bitter gourd, *Karela*
Broccoli, *Vilayati Gobhi*
Celery, *Ajmoda*
China grass, *Chini ghaas*
Cranberries, *Karaunda*
Cucumber, *Kheera*
Curry leaves, *Curry patta*
Daikon, *Mooli*
Dandelion, *Kukraundha*
Dill, *Suwa*
Dried limes, *Sukha nimbu*
Eggplant, *Baigan*
Endive, *Salad ka patta*
French green beans, *Faras bean*
Garlic chive, *Lahsoon ka patta*
Ginger, *Adrak*
Green Pea, *Mutter*
Kohlrabi, *Bandgobi*
Leeks, Gandana, *Vilayati piyaz*
Mint, *Pudina*
Mushroom, *Khumbi*
Okra, *Bhindi*
Parsley, *Ajamoda*
Pumpkin, *Kaddu*
Sage, *Salvia or Sefakuss*
Seaweed, *Samudri Shaival*
Shallots, *Choti Pyaz*
Spinach, *Palak*
Spring Onion, *Hara piyaz*
Sweet potato, *Shakarkandi*
Turnip, *Shalgam*
Watercress, *Jalkumbhi*
Zucchini, *Turai*

Others

Mixed fresh herbs, a combination of thyme, sage, mint or any other herbs locally available
Mixed berries, strawberries, red raspberries, blackberries and blue berries and/or any other locally available berries
Guacamole, avocado based sauce
Sev, long thread like noddles shredded into small bits made of gram flour and deep-fried until crisp
Tahini, a paste made from ground, hulled sesame seeds
Tamari, a type of soy sauce made without wheat, having a rich flavour

Getting Started: Tips and Basic Recipes

Basic Herbs and Spices for Ayurvedic Cooking

Herbs and spices are essential in Ayurveda; they stimulate the appetite and increase our ability to digest what we eat, increasing our overall health and well-being. Here is a list of basics herbs and spices you should keep on hand in your cabinet. See the Food Guidelines Chart in the Appendix (page 223) for information on what herbs and spices are appropriate for each *dosha*.

Dry: Bay leaves; black pepper; cardamom, ground and whole (pods); cayenne pepper; chilies, red; cinnamon sticks; cloves, whole; coriander, ground; cumin, ground and whole; curry leaves; fennel seeds; fenugreek; garam masala; mustard seeds, black; mustard seeds, crushed and whole; turmeric

Fresh: Coriander; chilies, green; garlic; ginger

Fresh is Always Best

Just as freshly ground coffee has more aroma and flavour, the same goes for your ingredients. The fresher the spices, the more flavourful your food will be. I recommend keeping a coffee grinder on hand just for your spices. Grind them as you need them just as you would with coffee. Ground spices will keep for 4-6 months in a spice rack. To clean the coffee grinder, grind ½ slice of bread into breadcrumbs, then discard.

Garam Masala

Garam masala (which means 'hot spices') is a traditional blend of dried spices that can be used in the same way as black pepper or other seasonings. It is a warming food which also stimulates digestion and circulation. For seasoning, only a little is needed, e.g., ¼-½ tsp.

To make garam masala: 5 cinnamon sticks, broken, ¼ cup cardamom pods with seeds, ¼ cup black peppercorns and ⅛ cup cloves. To break cinnamon sticks, place between a folded dishcloth and crush with a hammer or a rolling pin. Preheat oven to 95°C. Sprinkle ingredients evenly on a baking sheet. Roast for 20-30 minutes, stirring from time to time to ensure they do not brown. Remove from oven and allow the mixture to cool. Or heat a *tawa* and roast all the ingredients for 8-10 minutes. Break open each cardamom pod by squeezing between thumb and forefinger. Place cardamom seeds in mixture and discard pods. In a coffee grinder (not one usually used for coffee), grind ingredients until they become a fine powder. Store in an airtight container.

Good Oils and Good Fats

Oils are the main source of good, healthy fats in our diets. In general, choose oils that are expeller-pressed, which are those that have been extracted from seeds or nuts through a chemical-free mechanical process; or cold-pressed oils, which are expeller-pressed in a heat-controlled environment of less than 49°C. Unrefined oils — oils left in their virgin state after pressing — are very rich in nutrients, but when used for cooking, they have a lower smoke point (the temperature at which oil begins to decompose and give off fumes). Some types of oils maybe stored in the refrigerator after they have been opened to extend their shelf life and maintain their nutritional value.

Here are the 'good oils' I recommend; use organic versions wherever possible:

- **Coconut oil** has a good flavour and is full of nutrients that are retained at high temperatures.

- **Flax seed oil,** like hemp oil, is full of essential omega-3 fatty acids. Use unheated, and add it to shakes, salad dressings, cereals, or toast. Refrigerate after opening and use within 6 weeks.
- **Ghee** Use sparingly if you are trying to lose weight. It is very calming to the nervous system. For great flavour and to calm Vata, use a little *ghee* mixed with olive oil when sautéing. Ghee can be stored at room temperature.
- **Grapeseed oil** maintains its healthy properties at high temperatures. Use sparingly if you are trying to lose weight.
- **Hemp oil,** like flax seed oil, is full of the essential omega-3 fatty acids and should be used unheated, such as in shakes and salad dressings. Refrigerate after opening and use within 6 weeks.
- **Olive oil** is an all-purpose oil as it is readily available and cooks well at high heat without losing its nutritional value. Also use in salads, soups, and sauces.
- **Sesame oil** is another healthy oil. I recommend using only high quality versions. Sesame oil is more expensive, but you only need to use a little for wonderful flavour.

'Good fats,' an essential part of our diet, can be found in olives, avocados, almonds, walnuts, pistachios, and other nuts and seeds. The key to health is to consume these good fats and oils in moderation. A diet too low in fat can lead to attention deficit disorder, heart disease, cancer, autoimmune disorders, skin and joint problems, premenstrual problems, and depression and other mood disorders. On the flipside, a diet too high in fat (particularly 'bad' fats) can lead to obesity, cancer, and heart disease.

Trans fats are the worst of the 'bad fats'; they clog up arteries and impair blood flow, which increases the risk of heart attacks and strokes. Trans fats are most often found in junk food, so it is best to avoid virtually almost all fast, fried, and processed foods, including instant and frozen foods. If you don't have enough time to cook, go to a health food store or local market and pick up something quick and healthy. Always read the package label so you know what you are putting in your body. Avoid trans fats as much as possible; this includes products that have hydrogenated or partially hydrogenated fats such as monoglycerides and diglycerides.

Ghee

Clarified butter, also known as *ghee*, is butter with the milk solids removed. Ghee is a digestive aid that improves the absorption of nutrients from food it's used with. It is also known to improve memory, lubricate the connective tissues, and act as a catalytic agent to carry the medicinal properties of herbs to the body. Ghee calms both Pitta and Vata, but should be used sparingly by Kapha and those who have high cholesterol or suffer from obesity, and when you want to detoxify (i.e. when you are on a cleanse). Ghee doesn't need to be refrigerated as the impurities have been removed.

To make ghee: In a pot on medium heat, melt 500 g unsalted butter completely (watch carefully to ensure it doesn't burn). Bring to a boil and skim off any foam, then reduce heat to low. Stir occasionally for 15-20 minutes. When the whitish curds turn light brown, it is ready. Skim off any additional foam, then pour through a sieve or cheesecloth into a glass container with a tight lid to store. Discard the curds at the bottom of the pan.

Paneer

Paneer is homemade cheese, similar in taste to Ricotta and cottage cheese, but its souring process makes it easier to digest. You can sauté paneer before adding to vegetable dishes, an easy way to add protein. Paneer is similar to tofu in texture as well as its ability to absorb flavours around it. In fact, you may substitute tofu in all the recipes that call for paneer.

To make paneer: Take 8 cups whole milk, 6 tbsp plain yogurt and 1½ tsp lemon juice, strained through a fine sieve. In a large heavy pot on high heat, bring milk to a boil (watch closely to ensure it does not burn).

In the Ayurvedic tradition, bringing milk to a boil, then cooling it, makes it easier to digest. Often those who have a low tolerance for dairy find that they can enjoy it again when they follow this practice. Boiling it also sterilizes it without destroying its nutritional properties.

As soon as foam begins to rise, remove pot from heat. Add yogurt and lemon juice and mix well. The curds will start to solidify and separate from the liquid whey. Over a bowl, strain the mixture through a piece of cheesecloth, reserving the curds (paneer) in the cheesecloth. Wrap the cloth tightly around the curds, squeezing out the excess liquid.

Place the paneer, still wrapped in the cheesecloth, on a cutting board, and another board or baking sheet on top of it. Weight it down with about 7 kg of heavy jars or cans and let sit at room temperature for 6-8 hours, until cheese is firm. Unwrap and cut into 2-cm cubes. Cover and refrigerate until ready to use. Makes 6-8 servings.

Sprouting Beans and Lentils

Sprouting beans and lentils increases their digestibility and significantly increases their nutritional value. This process breaks proteins and carbs into easily digestible amino acids, starches, and sugars. Sprouted beans are a rich source of protein, vitamins, and minerals, making them known as a super food. Here is a basic way to sprout beans and lentils to create a very nourishing and gentle food.

In a large bowl or pot of water, soak 2 cups beans or lentils overnight. In the morning, drain and rinse in a colander. Set colander over bowl or pot to aerate and cover with a clean damp dishcloth. Leave in indirect light. In the evening, rinse again, thoroughly. Once again, drain over bowl or pot and cover with damp dishcloth. Repeat the next morning and evening. By then, they will start to sprout little tails. When tails are about ¼-in (½-cm) long, store in an airtight container and refrigerate for up to 4 days or use immediately.

Cooking Beans and Lentils

Here is a general recipe for cooking most beans and lentils. You should use about 1 cup beans or lentils for every 3-4 cups of water for cooking. Keep in mind that the longer you soak the beans and lentils, the less cooking time they require.

Take 1 cup beans or lentils, 2-3 cups water (for soaking), 3-4 cups water (for cooking), ¼ tsp turmeric, 1 tsp salt, 2 slices ginger, 1 green chili, slit at end (optional), 1 tsp good oil and ⅛ tsp asafoetida (optional). In a large pot or bowl, soak beans or lentils overnight in water for no more than 12 hours; lentils require a minimum of 4 hours. Drain soaked beans or lentils. In a large pot, combine water and beans or lentils and bring to a boil. A froth may rise to the surface; skim off as much as possible with a slotted spoon. Add all remaining ingredients. Reduce heat to simmer; make sure there is always enough water to prevent drying or burning. Beans or lentils are done when the center is tender, but not mushy. Discard ginger, and chili (if using) before serving.

Additional Tips for Cooking Beans and Lentils

- Make sure ng process so some people add the salt at the end.
- Cooking pulses with fresh ginger aids their digestibility, as does adding asafoetida.
- Simmering means liquid continues to bubble occasionally. This usually requires medium or medium-low heat, however you should always adjust the heat to ensure bubbling is at its lowest point.
- Removing the froth that appears on the surface helps to prevent flatulence.

Tips for Cooking Rice

- Wash rice by rinsing in water and draining 3 times; any more than this and you'll lose nutrients.
- An easy way to measure water for your rice is to make sure it covers the rice by (2½-cm).
- Use a pot with a tightly fitting lid as this allows the rice to cook in its own steam; and try not to peek, as this will slow the cooking process!

Delicious Choices Recipes

What the Symbols Mean

Each recipe includes the three *dosha* symbols:

Ⓥ Vata Ⓟ Pitta Ⓚ Kapha

as well as information on how the specific recipe affects each *dosha*:

[+]	means that the recipe increases the qualities of the *dosha* and may aggravate you.
[slightly +]	means that the recipe slightly increases the qualities of the *dosha* and may aggravate if you have this in excess.
[Ø]	means that the recipe has a neutral effect on the *dosha*.
[−]	means that the recipe balances or decreases the qualities of the *dosha*.

Recipes may also include ingredient modifications to help calm specific *doshas*; e.g., a recipe such as *Buckwheat Pancakes* (page 37) slightly increases Kapha, but substituting the banana with grated apple will reduce Kapha and thus make the recipe better for those whose primary *dosha* is Kapha. (For more ideas on modifying recipes to suit your *dosha*, see the Food Guidelines Chart on page 223)

Ⓓ Some recipes have a tridoshic symbol, meaning they are appropriate and calming for all three *doshas*.

Remember, don't let the recipes intimidate you! Be open to experimenting, listen to your body, and discover how good you'll feel by cooking the Ayurvedic way.

Eating breakfast is important, given that we fast all night; it keeps the blood sugar level balanced. Try to use the best breakfast ingredients you can find (e.g., free range eggs, home-made almond milk, fresh breads right for your body type). I have included both lighter and heavier breakfasts, depending on your mood and appetite.

Breakfast

If you are a Vata, you will probably want to have something grounding and comforting with good carbs, such as *Porridge with Stewed Berries* (page 41). If you are a Kapha, you may want something like the *Indian Omelette* (page 50). But Kaphas may not want to eat until mid-morning so make sure you take something healthy with you to eat then, like a fruit salad. If you are a Pitta, you may wake up so intent on your day's goals that you think you can skip breakfast, yet it will be the most important thing you do in your day; at least make a shake and take it with you. It is always important to listen to your body's needs. The health and well-being of your body will reflect in your day.

slightly slightly

−Ⓥ +Ⓟ +Ⓚ

Fresh Fruit Salad with Yogurt & Flax Seeds

This fruit salad, a delicious and fresh way to start the day, includes essential omega oils to fuel the brain.

2 cups strawberries, sliced
2 cups blueberries
2 bananas, sliced
- *To reduce Kapha: substitute 2 cups sliced apricots*

2 tbsp flax seeds, ground
- *To reduce Pitta: use 2 tbsp hemp oil*

2 cups plain yogurt (may use vanilla-flavoured yogurt)
Mint leaves (for garnish)
1 strawberry (for garnish)

In a large bowl, combine fruit, flax seeds, and yogurt. Garnish with mint leaves and strawberry.

Makes **4 servings.**

slightly

–(V) –(P) +(K)

Buckwheat Pancakes

These nourishing and delicious pancakes digest well and make you feel just as good as they taste!

½ cup buckwheat flour
½ tsp baking powder
½ a banana, mashed
- *To reduce Kapha: substitute with ¾ cup grated apple*

½ cup soy milk (enough to mix batter)
1 tsp *ghee* (or coconut oil)
Apple sauce

In a large bowl, combine flour and baking powder and stir. Add banana and soy milk, and beat until mixture has become a smooth liquid. In a frying pan on medium-high heat, melt *ghee* and spread evenly over surface. Pour batter into rounds, about ⅓ cup of batter for each small pancake. When batter starts to bubble, flip to cook other side until golden brown. Serve with apple sauce.

Multiply the amount of each ingredient by the number of desired servings.

Makes **1 serving.**

−Ⓥ øⓅ øⓀ

Simply Delicious Crêpes

½ cup brown rice flour
¼ tsp salt
1 egg
⅓ cup milk
⅓ cup water
1 tsp coconut oil

Breakfast never tasted so good! This is a basic recipe for crêpes; be creative with fillings. Try applesauce, baked bananas, cooked berries, or maple syrup.

In a medium bowl, combine flour and salt. In a small bowl, beat egg. Add egg to flour mixture and stir until well mixed. Add milk and water gradually while continuing to mix until smooth. In a small frying pan on medium-high heat, heat coconut oil evenly over pan. Add ¼ cup of batter and tilt frying pan so that it spreads evenly. When crêpe bubbles and its underside is golden brown, flip and brown the other side. Remove and set aside on a plate. Repeat with remaining batter. If needed, heat additional coconut oil.

Makes **2 servings.**

slightly slightly

–Ⓥ +Ⓟ +Ⓚ

South Indian Dosas

1½ cups rice flour
1 cup *urad dal* flour
½ tsp salt
¼ tsp fenugreek
2 cups water
6 tsp coconut oil

***Dosas* are rice flour crêpes that are a South Asian breakfast specialty. They are sour and should be eaten with lentils. To reduce Kapha or Pitta, I recommend the *Strengthening Tur Dal* (page 118). Serve in the traditional manner with *Coconut Mint Chutney* (page 175).**

In a medium bowl, combine all ingredients except the oil. You may need to add an additional ¼ cup water to make a semi-thin paste (i.e. crêpe mixture). The longer this mixture soaks, the more tart it becomes.

In a large frying pan on medium-high heat, melt ½ tsp of the oil evenly over surface. Add ¼ cup of the batter and tilt the pan so that it spreads evenly. Spread another ½ tsp oil at the edges and on top of *dosa*. When bottom is golden brown, flip and brown the other side. Roll dosa and place on a plate. Repeat with remaining batter.

Makes **6 servings.**

Urad dal *is warm and heavy, and very beneficial and nourishing for Vata in small amounts.*

−(V) +(P) +(K)

Breakfast Rice

This instant and flavourful breakfast is great for using up extra rice and almonds left over from making *Almond Milk* (page 186). Vata, Kapha, and Pitta may use Basmati rice cooked *al dente*.

- 2 cups organic short grain brown rice, cooked
- 1 cup plain yogurt
- 2 tbsp honey
- 2 pinch of ground cardamom
- ¼ cup crushed almonds

In a medium bowl, combine rice and yogurt and stir. Add honey and cardamom and mix well. Sprinkle with crushed almonds and serve.

To make a savory version of this recipe, omit honey and ground cardamom and add salt and freshly ground pepper — my favourite.

Makes **2 servings.**

slightly
–(V) –(P) +(K)

Porridge with Stewed Berries

This porridge is a great way to get both your fruit and grains. It's like eating dessert in the morning! It includes your essential omegas, too.

1 cup porridge oats
2 cups water
¼ tsp salt
¾ cup mixed berries
1 tbsp flax seeds
- *To reduce Pitta: substitute with hemp oil or omit*

1 tsp sweetener
1 cup soy milk

In a pot on medium heat, combine porridge oats, water, and salt. Bring to a boil then reduce to a simmer. Add berries and cook until done, about 7-10 minutes. Sprinkle with flax seeds, add sweetener and milk, and serve.

Makes **1-2 servings.**

slightly

–(V) –(P) +(K)

Multi-grain Cereal Breakfast

1 cup multi-grain cereal
2 tbsp bran
1 tbsp flax seeds, ground
- *To reduce Pitta: omit and add 1 tbsp hemp oil just before serving*

1 tbsp walnuts, roughly crushed
2 cups milk
- *To reduce Kapha: use goat's milk*

½ cup fresh berries

My brother Vijay and his wife Sona lived in Germany where they created this lighter version of Bavarian muesli, which is usually prepared with heavy cream. Tasty and full of fibre, this recipe is everything you need to start your day. Make it as soon as you get up and by the time you are ready for breakfast, it will be waiting for you.

In a medium bowl, combine all ingredients except berries and let sit for 20-30 minutes. Just before serving, add berries.

Makes **1-2 servings.**

–Ⓥ +Ⓟ –Ⓚ

Breakfast Stir Fry

1 tsp olive oil
1 tsp toasted sesame oil
½ cup broccoli florets and stems, chopped
½ cup celery, chopped
¼ cup yellow bell peppers, chopped
¼ cup red bell peppers, chopped
¼ cup cashew nuts
- *To reduce Kapha and Pitta: omit*

Dash of soy sauce
Dash of chili sauce
- *To reduce Pitta: omit*

Dash of oyster sauce
1 cup tofu, cubed

Do you ever wake up in the morning and want something savory, energizing, and filling, with some protein to carry you through the day? I felt like that one morning and created this. It hit the spot and now it has become a staple for me. I recommend using tofu that has been marinated in something tasty, a flavour you like.

In a wok or frying pan on medium-high, heat oils. Add all vegetables and cashew nuts, and sauté for a few minutes. Add dashes of all three sauces. Cover with lid to let veggies steam for about 2 minutes. Add tofu and stir to mix well. Cook for another minute. Serve immediately.

Makes **2 servings.**

-Ⓥ -Ⓟ -Ⓚ
Ⓓ

Tofu Scramble

1 tsp *ghee*
1 tbsp onions, chopped (optional)
1 tbsp coriander leaves, chopped (or parsley)
¼ cup tomatoes, diced
¼ tsp green chilies, minced
¼ tsp turmeric
Salt to taste
2 cups tofu, crumbled
1 tsp water

This is a wonderful dish as the tofu absorbs all the flavours, so it's very tasty. If possible, use frozen, left-over tofu as it easily crumbles. I like to serve this with a glass of almond milk for extra protein and natural oils.

In a medium frying pan on medium heat, melt *ghee*. Add all ingredients except tofu and water and sauté for 2 minutes. Add tofu and water and sauté for another 2-3 minutes, until most liquid has been absorbed.

Makes **2-4 servings.**

–Ⓥ –Ⓟ –Ⓚ
Ⓓ

Tofu Veggie Breakfast Wrap

A great breakfast that can be easily packed to eat on the go.

1 tbsp extra-virgin olive oil
½ onion, sliced finely lengthwise
¾ cup red bell peppers, sliced finely lengthwise
½ cup broccoli florets and stems, chopped
⅓ cup tofu, cubed or crumbled
Salt and freshly ground pepper to taste
¼ tsp turmeric
Chili sauce to taste
- *To reduce Pitta: omit*

2 Whole grain chapatis (page 150)
4 slices cheese
- *To reduce Kapha: omit*

¼ cup coriander leaves, chopped

In a large frying pan on medium-high, heat the oil. Add onions, peppers, and broccoli and sauté for 2 minutes, stirring frequently. Cover with lid and reduce heat to medium-low allowing veggies to cook in their own steam for 2-3 minutes. Add tofu, salt, pepper, and chili sauce and sauté on medium heat for another 2 minutes until tofu has absorbed most of the liquid. Remove pan from heat.

In a medium pan on medium heat arrange the chapatis. Place two cheese slices down the centre of each chapati. As soon as cheese is melted, remove chapatis from pan and set each on a plate. Place ½ tofu filling down the center of each chapati, leaving at least 4-cm at the bottom empty. Sprinkle coriander leaves on top of filling. Fold bottom up to form an envelope base and roll chapati sides up.

Makes **2 servings.**

–Ⓥ +Ⓟ øⓀ

Spicy Scrambled Tofu

Very tasty; beware, these could get addictive. Turmeric is a natural antibiotic and blood cleanser. Cumin aids the digestion, ginger warms the body, coriander pacifies all the *doshas*, and chilies add kick to your metabolism.

5 cups tofu
3 tbsp milk or water
½ tsp salt
¼ tsp freshly ground pepper
1 tbsp oil
1 tbsp onions, minced
1 tsp fresh ginger, minced
2 tbsp coriander leaves, chopped
¼ tsp turmeric
1½ tsp fresh green chilies, minced
- *To reduce Pitta: omit*

½ tsp ground cumin

In a medium bowl, crumble tofu. Add milk, salt, and pepper and mix well. Set aside. In a frying pan on medium-high, heat oil. Add onions and ginger and sauté for 1 minute. Add coriander leaves, turmeric, and green chilies. Mix well. Reduce heat to low and pour in tofu. Cook for 3-4 minutes. Serve immediately.

Makes **3-4 servings.**

Variation:

- Substitute tofu with 6 eggs and use milk instead of water.

–Ⓥ +Ⓟ øⓀ
Ⓓ

Sweet French Toast

A sweet yet filling breakfast, and the strawberries and mint make it a special treat.

5 eggs
- *To reduce Pitta and Kapha: use 2 eggs and 5 egg whites*

Pinch of salt
1 tbsp water
4 slices bread, your choice
- *To reduce Kapha: use rye or millet bread*

4 tsp *ghee* (or good oil, page 27)
8 strawberries, quartered
4 tbsp honey
Sprigs of mint (for garnish)

In a large bowl, combine eggs, salt, and water and beat until frothy. Dip a slice of bread in the bowl, letting it soak up ¼ of the egg mixture, covering evenly. In a frying pan on medium-high heat, melt 1 tsp of *ghee*. Fry bread until lightly brown on each side, 1-2 minutes. Repeat until all 4 slices are done. Serve with strawberries and honey. Garnish with mint.

Makes **2-4 servings.**

slightly

−Ⓥ +Ⓟ øⓀ

Eggs with Turmeric & Parsley

4 eggs
- *To reduce Pitta and Kapha: use 2 eggs and 4 egg whites*

1 tbsp water
1 tbsp *ghee* (or good oil, page 27)
¼ cup onions, minced
½ cup tomatoes, chopped
2 tbsp parsley, chopped
¼ tsp turmeric
Salt and freshly ground pepper to taste
Pinch of cayenne pepper
- *To reduce Pitta: omit*

Another tasty, nutritious way to eat your eggs. The *ghee* calms Vata while the turmeric acts as a natural antibiotic and blood cleanser. The cayenne speeds up the metabolism, which is excellent for reducing Kapha. Parsley is cooling for Pitta and an excellent source of iron.

In a bowl, combine eggs and water and beat, then set aside. In a frying pan on medium-high, heat *ghee*. Stir in onions and sauté for 1 minute; add tomatoes and sauté for another minute. Stir in parsley and sauté for another 30 seconds, mixing well. Pour in eggs and add turmeric, salt, pepper, and cayenne. Gently lift eggs when the bottom sets so eggs are cooked through. Cook for an additional 2 minutes until eggs no longer runny. Serve immediately.

When making this recipe, make sure to watch your heat settings. Reduce heat if it gets too hot as this dish can easily burn.

Makes **2-4 servings.**

–Ⓥ +Ⓟ +Ⓚ

Immi's Scrambled Eggs

- 4 eggs
- 2 tsp tomato purée
- Salt and freshly ground pepper to taste
- 1-2 tsp red chili flakes
- 2 tbsp milk
- 1 cup cheese, crumbled
- 2 tbsp *ghee* (or butter)

My cousin Immi, who lives in Scotland, claims that this recipe cures hangovers. He says the chilies are the key. (This makes sense in Ayurveda, as the Pitta-increasing chilies help to reduce the Kapha state.) He recommends two eggs per person.

In a large bowl, beat eggs. Add all other ingredients except *ghee*, and whisk with a fork until well mixed. Set aside. In a frying pan on medium heat, melt *ghee* evenly over the pan. Pour in egg mixture, constantly stirring and folding until the eggs are cooked through. (Immi recommends that you leave these eggs slightly soft and runny.) Serve immediately.

Makes **2 servings.**

–(V) +(P) ø(K)

Indian Omelette

An Indian breakfast favourite on weekends. Save leftovers to cut into triangles for snacks or a late lunch. Serve with chapatis or your favourite toast.

6 eggs
- *To reduce Pitta and Kapha: use 3 eggs and 6 egg whites*

2 tbsp water
Salt and freshly ground pepper to taste
1 tbsp *ghee* (or good oil, page 27)
- *To reduce Kapha: use a light oil*

½ cup red onions, chopped
2 tsp green chilies
- *To reduce Pitta: use ½ tsp*

½ cup coriander leaves, chopped

In a large bowl, combine eggs and water and beat until frothy. Add salt and pepper to taste. In a large frying pan on medium-high, melt *ghee* evenly over pan. Add onions, chilies, and coriander and sauté until onions are softened. Pour in egg mixture, spreading evenly over the frying pan. Reduce heat to medium. Lift eggs gently with a spatula to ensure that eggs are cooked through. Cover with a lid and gently steam for a minute or two, checking to make sure it does not burn. Serve immediately.

Makes **3-4 servings.**

Two key principles of an Ayurvedic diet are
a) eat balanced meals, and
b) avoid snacking.
Snacks, however, are a great way to avoid blood sugar highs and lows, which can tamper with our metabolisms and make us feel exhausted.

Appetizers, Snacks & Dips

In this section I have included some tasty, nutrient-filled snacks that will stop you from reaching for that next cup of coffee or biscuit in a desperate attempt to get through the day. Many are easy to carry to work, like the *Potato Tikis* (page 62) or the *Savory Dhokla Squares* (page 65). *Spiced Almonds* (page 69) are easy to keep on hand for those sudden low-energy moments. There are also a number of fabulous and healthy appetizers that are great openings to any meal.

slightly
−Ⓥ +Ⓟ +Ⓚ

Soothing Guacamole

This is a quick, delicious, and nutritious appetizer or snack, filled with the essential fatty acids and protein of the avocado. It is a calming dish that reduces Vata. The garlic adds a nice punch to the recipe.

¼ tsp green chilies, or to taste
- *To reduce Pitta: omit*

1 clove garlic
- *To reduce Pitta: omit*

2 tbsp coriander leaves
½ cup tomatoes, chopped
- *To reduce Pitta: omit*

1 cup avocado, chopped
Juice of ½ a lemon
Salt to taste

In a blender or food processor, combine chilies, garlic, and coriander and blend until finely chopped. Add tomatoes, avocado, lemon juice, and salt and blend until the mixture is quite smooth, but still has some chunks of tomato.

Makes **1½ servings.**

Don't rinse out the delectable remainders in your blender; instead, use them to make Yogurt Guacamole Lassi. Once you have transferred your guacamole to a bowl, add 1 tbsp plain yogurt and 200 ml water to the blender or food processor and blend again. Pour in a glass and enjoy!

slightly
+(V) –(P) +(K)

Four-Layer Bean Dip

One of my close friends often makes this for potluck dinners where it is always a hit. Serve with your favourite chips, or bread.

- 2 cups avocados, mashed
- 1 tbsp lemon juice
- ½ tsp salt
- ¼ tsp freshly ground pepper
- 1 cup sour cream
  - *To reduce Kapha: use a light version*
- ½ cup mayonnaise
- ½ cup spring onions, chopped
- 2 cups tomatoes, chopped
  - *To reduce Pitta: omit*
- ½ cup black olives, pitted and chopped
- 2 cups cheddar cheese, grated
  - *To reduce Pitta and Kapha: use Mozzarella*
- 1½ cups boiled and mashed beans

In a bowl, combine avocados, lemon juice, salt, and pepper and mix well, then set aside. In another bowl, combine sour cream and mayonnaise and mix well, then set aside. In a third bowl, combine green onions, tomatoes, olives, and cheese. Stir together, then set aside. In a pan, spread beans evenly over the bottom. Then spread avocado mixture over beans, and follow with sour cream mixture, and cheese mixture.

Makes **8 servings.**

Avocados are a cholesterol-free food. For every 30 g of avocado, there are 5 g of fat, but it is monounsaturated, often called the 'good fat.' Avocados are rich in B vitamins, folic acid, and antioxidants that aid our bodies in the elimination of 'free radicals,' or disease-causing toxins known as ama in Ayurveda.

slightly slightly
+(V) +(P) +(K)

Eggplant Dip

The secret to this recipe is ensuring that the eggplant is well cooked before you mash and blend it with the other ingredients. It is hard to believe how simple and delicious this dish is!

2 large eggplants
1 tbsp olive oil
- *To reduce Vata: add extra tbsp oil*

1 clove garlic
4 tbsp lemon juice
¾ tsp salt, or to taste
1 tbsp tahini

Set oven to broil. Rub both eggplants with olive oil until they are shiny. With a fork, pierce holes all over eggplants. Broil for at least 40 minutes, turning each once, until eggplants are soft and wrinkled. Remove from oven and let cool. Peel off skin and discard. In a medium bowl, mash eggplant flesh until it is pulpy. In a blender or food processor, pulse garlic until minced. Add eggplant and all remaining ingredients, pulsing until smooth.

To reduce Kapha and Vata, add ½ tsp *Coriander Mint Chutney* (page 175); to reduce Pitta, add 1 tbsp freshly chopped mint leaves.

Makes **6 servings.**

slightly
–(V) –(P) +(K)

Spinach Dip

Spinach — which is healing for the lungs and liver — is good for all *doshas*. It also helps to reduce Kapha. This dip is a delectable way to get some of your daily intake of greens. I've always loved spinach dip, but I find many versions are too heavy. Serve with fresh veggies to reduce Kapha.

5 cups spinach, roughly chopped
2 cloves garlic
2 tbsp green onions, chopped
½ green chili, or to taste
- *To reduce Pitta: omit*

¼ cup parsley
¼ cup coriander leaves
1 tbsp lemon juice
Salt and freshly ground pepper to taste
2 cups light sour cream
- *To reduce Vata: use a full-fat version*

¼ cup light mayonnaise
- *To reduce Vata: use a full-fat version*

In a medium pot of water on high heat, bring to a boil and add spinach. Cover with lid and blanch for 2-3 minutes, until spinach is wilted. Drain and set aside.

In a blender or food processor, pulse garlic, green onions, and chili until minced. Add parsley and coriander and pulse for a few seconds. Add spinach, then pulse again. Add all remaining ingredients and blend until just mixed.

Makes **2½ cups.**

slightly slightly
+(V) +(P) −(K)

Baked Pakoras

Pakoras, also known as *bhajias*, are tasty vegetable bites coated in a gram flour batter. Traditionally they are deep-fried, but this is a baked version that can be eaten guilt-free. Pakoras are best served with *Taramind Chutney* (page 174), but they can also be served with hot chili sauce, Coconut Mint Chutney (page 175), or *Coriander Mint Chutney* (page 173).

1½ cups gram flour
¾ tsp ground cumin
½ tsp ginger, grated or minced
½ tsp garlic, crushed or minced
1 tsp green chilies, minced
1 tsp salt, or to taste
1 cup plain yogurt
About 4-5 cups spinach, chopped
½ tsp baking powder
Olive oil spray
½ cup *Tamarind Chutney*

Preheat oven to 180°C. In a large bowl, combine flour, cumin, ginger, garlic, chilies, salt, and yogurt and beat with a wooden spoon until well mixed. Stir in spinach and baking powder. Pour mixture into a lightly-oiled pan. Cover with foil and bake for about 70 minutes. Test with a toothpick; if it comes out clean, it's done. Cut into slices, lightly cover with olive oil spray, and place on a baking sheet. Increase oven heat to broil and place in oven for 4 minutes, flipping once, until slightly crisp and brown. (Watch carefully to ensure they do not burn.)

Makes **10 servings (2 per person).**

slightly

+(V) +(P) −(K)

Stuffed Mushroom Caps

I have been serving this recipe as a warm appetizer for years. These mushrooms are simple to make and pleasing to the palate.

12 large mushrooms
1 tsp *ghee* (or butter)
1 tsp olive oil
2 dry red chilies
- *To reduce Pitta: omit*

¼ cup onions, minced
2 cloves garlic, minced
⅓ cup parsley, minced
¼ cup cheese, grated

Preheat oven to 180°C. Remove stems from mushrooms and lay mushroom caps on a baking sheet, tops down. Finely chop stems and set aside. In a frying pan on medium-high, heat the *ghee* and oil. Add dry red chilies and sauté for about 1 minute, until chilies begin to blacken. Add onions and garlic and sauté for 1 minute. Add chopped mushroom stems and sauté for an additional 2 minutes. Cover with lid and continue to cook for another 3 minutes. Add parsley and cook for another 2 minutes, uncovered. Remove pan from heat. Let the mixture cool for 2-3 minutes. Stuff mushroom caps evenly with the cooked mixture and discard chilies. Sprinkle each stuffed mushroom cap with cheese and bake for 10 minutes until cheese has melted and starts to brown.

Makes **6 servings (2 per person).**

–Ⓥ øⓅ +Ⓚ

Banana Walnut Loaf

This is another delicious, never-fail recipe. I am addicted to banana bread, so I save a lot of money and calories while increasing my nutritional intake by making my own. Serve it on its own, or with fruit and frozen yogurt for dessert.

½ cup olive oil
¾ cup brown sugar (or ¼ cup jaggery and ½ cup brown sugar)
2 eggs
1¾ cups ripe bananas, mashed
¼ cup walnuts, chopped
1¼ cups whole wheat flour
¼ cup wheat germ
1 tsp vanilla extract
1 tbsp flax seeds, ground
1 tsp baking soda
1 tsp baking powder

Preheat oven to 180°C. In a large bowl, combine oil, sugar, eggs, bananas, and vanilla and stir until just mixed. Add flour, wheat germ, flax seeds, baking soda, and baking powder. Fold and combine until just moistened. Stir in chopped walnuts and pour into a lightly oiled 22 x 12 cm pan. Bake for 45 minutes to 1 hour, or until a toothpick or fork comes out clean.

Makes **6-8 servings.**

slightly
−(V) −(P) +(K)

Banana, Oat & Berry Muffins

Use ripe bananas for these low fat and healthy carb muffins.

1⅓ cups whole wheat flour
- *To reduce Kapha: use spelt flour*

1 tbsp flax seeds, ground
2 tbsp wheat germ
1 cup porridge oats
2 tsp baking powder
1 tsp baking soda
½ tsp salt
1 egg
¼ cup vegetable oil
¾ cup ripe bananas, mashed
- *To reduce Kapha: substitute additional 1 cup berries*

½ cup sweetener (e.g., brown sugar, maple syrup, honey)
- *To reduce Kapha: use honey*

¾ cup milk
½ cup mixed berries

Preheat oven to 205°C. In a large bowl, combine the first 7 ingredients, then mix and set aside. In a separate bowl, beat egg, then add oil, bananas, sweetener, and milk, and mix well. Add liquid ingredients to dry ingredients and mix to incorporate, then stir in berries. Lightly oil a muffin tin or cover with olive oil spray and spoon mixture evenly into muffin cups. Bake for 18-20 minutes, or until a toothpick or fork comes out clean. Let cool before serving.

Makes **12 muffins.**

+(V) −(P) −(K)

Blueberry Almond Muffins

1¾ cups barley flour
- *To reduce Vata: use spelt flour*

¾ tsp baking powder
¼ tsp baking soda
¼ tsp salt
1 tbsp lemon zest, packed
7 tbsp grapeseed oil (or canola oil)
½ cup sugar syrup
½ cup plain soy milk
½ tsp lemon juice
1 tsp vanilla extract
¾ cup blueberries
¼ cup almonds, peeled, toasted, and roughly chopped

The toasted almonds and the lemon zest combined with the blueberries and very little flour create a medley of flavours and textures. Soak almonds overnight to blanch them, then peel and toast them in the oven just before using. Soaking almonds increases their nutritional value as it returns the nut back to its live form.

Preheat oven to 180°C. In a bowl, sift together flour, baking powder, baking soda, and salt and set aside. In a separate bowl, whisk together all remaining ingredients except berries and almonds. Add berries and mix. Pour liquid mixture and mix well, then stir in almonds. Lightly oil a muffin pan and spoon mixture evenly into muffin cups. Bake for 15-18 minutes, or until a toothpick or fork comes out clean. Let cool.

Makes **12 muffins.**

Barley is a cool, light, and dry grain that alleviates Pitta and Kapha. Barley tea (¼ cup barley to 8 cups hot water) relieves fever and calms the urinary tract.

slightly
+(V) −(P) −(K)

Khandvi Rolls

Khandvi is a great afternoon pick-me-up and gets Kapha moving.

3 tbsp plain yogurt
1 cup water
1 cup gram flour
Salt to taste
¼ tsp turmeric
½ tsp cayenne pepper
3 tbsp lemon juice
2 cups water (for boiling)
3 tbsp olive oil
½ tsp black mustard seeds
½ tsp cumin seeds
1 tbsp sesame seeds
2 tbsp green chilies, finely chopped (for garnish)
- *To reduce Pitta: use only 1 chili or omit*

¼ cup coriander leaves, chopped (for garnish)

In a bowl, whisk together yogurt and water until smooth. In a separate bowl, combine flour, salt, turmeric, cayenne pepper and lemon juice. Add yogurt mixture to this bowl and mix until smooth.

In a large pot, bring 2 cups water to a boil. Reduce heat to simmer and add gram flour mixture. Stir frequently to ensure it does not stick to the bottom of the pan. Cook until mixture becomes a thick sauce. Remove from heat and spread onto a greased baking sheet (do this while the mixture is very hot). Leave to cool and dry out for about 15 min. Once cooled, cut into 4½-cm wide strips and roll lengthwise. Cut the rolls into 2½-cm wide pieces and place on serving platter.

In a small pot, heat oil. Add mustard seeds and cover with lid until they pop, about 30 seconds. Add cumin and sesame seeds. With a spoon, sprinkle seeds over rolls. Garnish with chopped green chilies and coriander.

Makes **8-12 rolls.**

slightly slightly

+(V) +(P) −(K)

Potato Tikis

These potato tikis are another all-time favourite of mine. They are easy to make for impromptu guests or as a quick snack. Serve with *Tamarind Chutney* (page 174) or a *green chutney*, and lemon wedges.

3 cups potatoes, boiled and mashed
1 tsp olive oil
4 tbsp lemon juice
¼ cup onions, minced
1 tsp green chilies, finely chopped, or to taste
- *To reduce Pitta: omit*

2 tbsp coriander leaves, chopped
1 tsp salt, or to taste
2 tbsp arrowroot
1 cup breadcrumbs
Olive oil spray

Preheat oven to 300°F (150°C). In a large bowl, combine all ingredients except eggs and breadcrumbs and mix well. Form dough into 12-14 balls 5-cm in diameter with hands and then flatten into 2½-cm thick tikis and set aside.

In a bowl mix 2 tbsp arrowroot with ½ cup water. In a separate bowl, place breadcrumbs.

Lightly cover baking sheet with olive oil spray. Dip each patty in arrowroot batter, then coat in breadcrumbs. Place patties on sheet and lightly cover with olive oil spray. Bake for 5 minutes, then turn tikis over and bake for 5 additional minutes, or until browned.

Makes **6-8 servings.**

–(V) –(P) –(K)
(D)

Papris

Kaphas should eat puris in moderation, no more than four per meal.

2/3 cup rice flour
2/3 cup spelt flour
1 tsp salt
3-9 tbsp cold water
Vegetable oil (for deep frying)

In a bowl, combine both flours and salt. Add 3 tbsp water and knead until dough can be gathered into a ball. If the dough is not yet sticky, add more water 1 tbsp at a time, until it is able to form a ball; be careful not to add more water than is needed. Knead dough for about 5 minutes until it is smooth and elastic. Again, gather dough into a ball, cover it with a sheet of wax paper, and let it sit for at least 30 minutes before rolling it out. On a lightly floured surface with a rolling pin, roll dough into a paper-thin sheet. Cut into 5-cm rounds with a cookie cutter or the rim of a glass. Transfer rounds onto a lightly floured clean, flat surface. Lay a damp tea towel over them to keep them from drying out.

In a deep frying pan or wok, heat 2-3 inches of oil until a drop of dough comes instantly to the surface. Deep-fry 8-10 puris at a time for 1-2 minutes, turning over frequently until they are golden brown on both sides. Remove with a slotted spoon onto a plate lined with paper towels.

Makes **75-80 puris.**

slightly
−Ⓥ +Ⓟ −Ⓚ

Bhel Tea Time Snack

Bhel is a favourite 'street food' and a special treat for guests. It looks festive and colourful when ingredients are served in individual bowls for guests to combine themselves on papris. Half the fun is putting them together to suit your personal taste.

3 cups puffed rice
1 onion, chopped
- *To reduce Pitta: omit*

2 tomatoes, diced
- *To reduce Pitta: omit*

2 cups potatoes, boiled and diced
- *To reduce Vata: omit*

3 tbsp coriander leaves, chopped
½ cup fine sev
2 cups *mung bean* sprouts, parboiled
¼ cup almonds, crushed
- *To reduce Kapha: omit*

1 lime, sliced into wedges
4 tbsp *green chutney*
- *To reduce Pitta: use version without chilies*

4 tbsp *Tamarind Chutney*
- *To reduce Pitta and Kapha: omit*

Salt to taste
10-12 *Papri*

Serve each ingredient (except papris) in separate bowls so guests can make their own combinations on a papri.

Another way to serve this snack is to add all ingredients except lime wedges and chutneys to a large bowl, toss, and serve with lime wedges and chutney on the side so guests can add their own.

Makes **5-6 servings (2 papris per person).**

Fine sev *is a snack that is made from gram flour and deep-fried until crisp. Salt and spices are added as flavouring.*

slightly
−Ⓥ −Ⓟ +Ⓚ

Savory Dhokla Squares

Someone discovered this fast and easy way to make an age-old Indian snack. Serve with *Tomato Chutney* (page 172), *green chutney* (page 173 or 175), or *chili sauce*. You may add a chopped green chili to batter, or sprinkle a little cayenne pepper on top once in baking dish to add flavour and colour. Pitta should omit.

1 cup cream of wheat
Salt to taste
1 tsp canola oil
- *To reduce Vata: use 2 tsp canola oil*

¼ tsp turmeric
½ tsp whole cumin seeds, crushed
1-2 tbsp coriander leaves, chopped
1½ tsp lemon juice
1 cup plain yogurt
¼ cup water
1 heaping tsp Eno Fruit Salt

In a large bowl, combine all ingredients except Eno and mix well. Pour batter into a shallow microwavable dish. Quickly stir in the Eno, which will start to activate immediately. Cut through batter with a knife or fork, immediately cover tightly with plastic wrap, and place in microwave on high for 8 minutes. Allow to sit for at least 4 minutes after cooking, then cut into diamond-shaped squares.

Makes **12-16 squares.**

slightly

−Ⓥ ØⓅ +Ⓚ

Papri Chat

This is another favourite savory street food snack.

1 cup potatoes, boiled and cubed
½ cup *Tamarind Chutney* (page 174)
4 tsp whole cumin seeds, toasted
3 green chilies, finely chopped
• *To reduce Pitta: omit*
½ cup plain yogurt, whipped up and runny
3 tsp cayenne pepper
12 *papris* (page 63)

Serve each ingredient (except papri) in separate bowls. You or your guests can pop a hole in a papri and stuff with 1 tsp diced potato, 1 tsp tamarind chutney, and a pinch each of cumin seeds and green chilies. Add 1 tsp yogurt sprinkled with a pinch of cayenne.

Makes **4-6 servings (2 or 3 papri per person).**

–(V) +(P) –(K)

Deviled Eggs with Green Chutney

My spicy version of the old favourite! A tasty way to get your daily protein.

4 hard-boiled eggs, peeled
2 tsp mayonnaise
- *To decrease Kapha: use light mayonnaise*

Salt to taste
2 tsp *green chutney*
- *To reduce Pitta: use version without chilies*

Coriander leaves, chopped (for garnish)
¼ tsp cayenne pepper (for garnish)

Cut eggs in half vertically and scoop out yolks, and place in a separate bowl. Add mayonnaise, salt, and chutney to yolks and mash with a fork. Fill egg white cavities with yolk mixture. Garnish with coriander leaves and sprinkle with cayenne.

Makes **4 servings (2 halves per person).**

−(V) −(P) +(K)

Green Chutney Cheese Toast

Nanistya, a friend from high school, became so addicted to this dish that once she moved to Montreal, my mother would make jars of chutney and send them to her!

4-6 slices of bread of your choice

Per slice:

1-2 tsp *green chutney* (page 173 or 175)
- *To reduce Pitta: use Coriander Mint Chutney* (page 175)

1 thin slice cheese
- *To reduce Vata: use cheddar*

Set oven to broil. Spread each slice of bread with chutney. Cover with slices of cheese. Place on a baking sheet and broil until cheese bubbles and starts to brown. (Watch carefully to ensure that they do not burn.)

Serve immediately or cut into squares and serve.

Makes **4-6 servings (1 slice per person).**

–Ⓥ –Ⓟ +Ⓚ

Spiced Almonds

Careful — these are addictive! Tree nuts — i.e. almonds, pecans, and walnuts — contain no cholesterol. Most of their calories come from unsaturated fats, or the essential fatty acids that our bodies need in small amounts. Although almonds generally increase Pitta, blanched almonds do not. Almonds are known to be 'brain food.' Remember, a ¼ cup serving is all you need!

1½ tsp ground cumin
1½ tsp salt
¼ tsp cayenne pepper, or more to taste
- *To reduce Pitta: omit*

1 large egg, white only
2½ cups almonds, blanched
Olive oil spray

Preheat oven to 150°C. In a small bowl, combine cumin, salt, and cayenne and set aside. In a bowl, beat egg white until frothy. Add spice mixture and almonds, and toss to mix well. Lightly cover a baking sheet with olive oil spray. Spread almonds out on baking sheet in a single layer. Bake for 25-30 minutes, stirring once or twice. Make sure almonds stay in a single layer. Remove from oven and cool. Store in a sealed container for up to 1 week.

Makes **2½ cups.**

slightly
−(V) +(P) +(K)

Spiced Pecans

Whenever we go on weekend getaways, my friend Nevenka brings these pecans, which give us the extra energy we need on our action-packed itineraries. Eat in small quantities.

¼ cup coconut oil
⅓ cup tamari or soy sauce
2 tsp ground ginger
¼ tsp cayenne pepper, or to taste
Olive oil spray
4 cups pecans

Preheat oven to 150°C. In a small pot over low heat, melt coconut oil. While oil is melting, in a small bowl, combine tamari, ginger, and cayenne and set aside. Lightly cover a baking sheet with olive oil spray or line with parchment paper. Spread pecans out on baking sheet in a single layer. Pour coconut oil over pecans and mix to coat. Bake for about 15 minutes. Remove from oven and immediately toss with tamari mixture. Return to oven and bake for 10 additional minutes. Remove from oven and cool at room temperature. Store in a sealed container.

Makes **4 cups.**

In Ayurveda, it is important to have at least some raw food like salad at every meal, as it aids digestion; the French have also known this for centuries, often referring to salad as 'the broom.' But raw food eaten alone can in fact be difficult to digest, especially for Vatas who should include some seasonal raw foods in their diet, but not as full meals, which are fine for Pittas and Kaphas.

Salads

Since summer is a Pitta season — hot and fiery — it is natural that all *doshas* enjoy more raw salads at this time to cool down. Leafy greens and herbs provide a bitter taste that brings out the sweetness and other contrasting flavours of the salad ingredients. In this section, I have included salads with cooked ingredients as well as an array of raw salads, which can be served as accompaniments to any dish, or as complete, balanced meals. At the end of this section are great salad dressings that add flavour to raw greens and vegetables and are a great source for good oils (e.g., flax or hemp oil), which are important to our diet and digestive health — Pitta and Kapha benefit from oils in small amounts. Dressings also provide a sour taste that is beneficial to all constitutions, but calms Vata the most.

slightly slightly

+(V) +(P) −(K)

Grated Beet & Broccoli Salad

This raw salad is rich in nutrients, textures, colours, and flavours. Pumpkin seeds are full of fiber, good oil, zinc, and iron, and are beneficial to all constitutions, but Vatas can eat more of these than Pittas and Kaphas. Pittas should reduce the amount of carrots and beets as they can be heating if consumed in excess.

1 medium-sized bowl mixed greens
1 cup sunflower seed sprouts, loosely packed
¾ cup carrots, grated
- *To reduce Pitta: ½ cup*

¼ cup beets, grated
- *To reduce Vata: 1 cup*

¼ cup broccoli chopped
1 tbsp dried cranberries
- *To reduce Vata: omit or substitute raisins*

1 tbsp raw pumpkin seeds
- *To reduce Vata: 2 tbsp*

¼ cup mint leaves, chopped
- *To reduce Pitta: ½ cup*

Dressing:
Juice of 1 lemon
4 tbsp hemp seed oil or olive oil
1 clove garlic, crushed
- *To reduce Pitta: omit*

1 tsp mustard
- *To reduce Pitta: omit*

Salt and freshly ground pepper to taste

In a medium bowl, combine all salad ingredients and toss. In a jar, combine all dressing ingredients and shake well. Pour over salad, toss again, and serve.

Makes **4-6 servings.**

+(V) −(P) −(K)

Refreshing Apple & Celery Salad

This is a crisp, light salad; the red apples make a lovely contrast with the green celery and red leaf lettuce. I often make this without the olive oil when I want to reduce Kapha. The lemon juice helps to bring out the sweetness of the apples.

6 cups red leaf lettuce, shredded
2 unpeeled red apples, diced (with peel showing decoratively)
2 stalks celery, sliced
½ cup walnuts, chopped
- *To reduce Kapha: use sunflower seeds*

Dressing:
6 tbsp lemon juice
4 tbsp olive oil
- *To reduce Kapha: omit*

In a medium bowl, combine all salad ingredients and toss. Drizzle with lemon juice and olive oil, toss again, and serve.

Makes **4-6 servings.**

–Ⓥ –Ⓟ –Ⓚ

The Essential Green Salad

I love getting my fibre from crisp greens and my essential fatty acids and protein from avocados. A good quality balsamic vinegar and olive oil define this salad. Add sunflower or pumpkin seeds or throw in some raisins or grapes to add more colour and texture to this salad.

4 cups mixed greens
1 avocado, sliced
1 cup cucumbers, sliced
- *To reduce Kapha: substitute celery*

1 cup broccoli florets, chopped
1 cup alfalfa sprouts

Dressing:
⅓ cup balsamic vinegar
¼ cup extra-virgin olive oil
Salt and freshly ground pepper to taste

In a large bowl, combine all salad ingredients and toss. Drizzle with balsamic vinegar and olive oil. Season with salt and pepper, toss again, and serve.

Makes **6 servings.**

+Ⓥ −Ⓟ −Ⓚ

Broccoli & Almond Salad

The almonds, red onions, and currants in this salad are a nice mixture of pungent and sweet tastes. Broccoli is a super cancer-fighting food. This is another good way to get your daily greens and fiber. This salad tastes wonderful after being chilled for a few hours, or overnight for the next day.

3 cups broccoli florets
½ cup red onions, chopped
- *To reduce Pitta: use ¼ cup or omit*

¼ cup almonds, chopped
½ cup currants

Dressing:
½ cup plain light yogurt
¼ cup light mayonnaise
2 tbsp honey
1 tbsp vinegar
Salt and freshly ground pepper to taste

In a medium bowl, combine all salad ingredients and toss. In a separate bowl, combine all dressing ingredients and mix well. Pour over salad and toss again. Adjust seasoning to taste, then serve.

Makes **4 servings.**

+(V) +(P) −(K)

Tomato & Yellow Bell Pepper Salad

Enjoy this colourful, crunchy medley! I love dishes like this that are quick, tasty, good-looking, and nutritious.

1 cup tomatoes, cubed
2 cups parsley, chopped
1 cup yellow bell peppers, cubed

Dressing:
2 tbsp balsamic vinegar or 3 tbsp lemon juice
2 tbsp olive oil (or flax or hemp oil)
Salt and freshly ground pepper to taste

In a medium bowl, combine all salad ingredients and toss. Drizzle with balsamic vinegar and oil. Season with salt and pepper, toss again, and serve.

Makes **4 servings.**

–(V) ø(P) +(K)

Mediterranean Breeze Salad

This salad is fabulously healthy as the mint is cooling and the tomatoes are packed with vitamin C.

1 cup tomatoes, chopped
1 cup avocado, chopped
¼ cup mint leaves, chopped
1 tbsp green onions, minced
2 tbsp lemon juice
2 tbsp olive oil (or flax or hemp oil)
1 tsp salt
¼ tsp cayenne pepper (optional)

In a large bowl, combine tomatoes, avocado, mint, and green onions and toss. Drizzle with lemon juice and oil. Sprinkle with salt and cayenne, toss again, and serve.

Makes **2 servings.**

slightly
−(V) +(P) −(K)

Fresh Radish & Endive Salad

1 radish cut into 5-cm-long sticks
- *To reduce Pitta: use half a radish*

A few sprigs dill (or mint leaves)
1½ cups cucumbers, cut into 5-cm-long sticks
2 cups carrots, cut into 5-cm-long sticks
1 bunch watercress leaves
2 heads of endive leaves, separated
Salt to taste
Juice of 1 lemon (or 4-6 tbsp rice vinegar)

This recipe includes mint or dill and endive, which are bitter, aiding digestion and cleansing the liver. Arrange artfully on a platter. As it is important to have some raw vegetables to accompany every meal to cleanse and balance the *doshas*, feel free to experiment! Select a variety of vegetables, sprinkling them with salt, lemon juice, or rice vinegar.

On a platter, arrange all ingredients except salt and lemon juice. Sprinkle with salt and lemon juice and serve.

Makes **6-8 servings.**

slightly

–Ⓥ +Ⓟ –Ⓚ

The Bittersweet Salad

I love the sweetness of the carrots with the bitter punch of the radish in this salad. It adds fiber and vitamins to a meal and cleanses the digestive system.

1 cup carrots, thinly sliced
1½ cups radish, thinly sliced
1 tsp salt
¼ cup rice vinegar
2 tbsp sweetener

In a colander, place carrots and radish and sprinkle with salt, then set over a sink or bowl to drain for 5-10 minutes. Rinse and gently squeeze excess water out of vegetables. In a jar, combine vinegar and sweetener and mix well until sweetener dissolves. In a serving bowl, combine vegetables and dressing and toss. Let sit for 15-30 minutes before serving.

Makes **4 servings.**

ØⓋ –Ⓟ –Ⓚ

Pomegranate & Spinach Salad

Pomegranates are an excellent source of antioxidants and strengthen the digestive tract. The pomegranate seeds add sweetness and colour, and are a delectable flavour combination with the spinach. When buying pomegranates, choose fruit that are blemish-free, brightly coloured, and heavy. Store them in a cool, dry place.

5-6 cups spinach leaves, chopped
⅓ cup coriander leaves, chopped
1 cup pomegranate seeds
⅓ cup pine nuts, toasted
¼ cup red onions, sliced (optional)
- *To reduce Pitta: omit*

Dressing:
4 tbsp olive oil
4 tbsp apple cider vinegar
2 tsp honey
Salt and freshly ground pepper to taste

In a large bowl, combine all salad ingredients and toss. In a jar, combine dressing ingredients and shake well. Pour dressing over salad, toss again, and serve.

Makes **4-5 servings.**

Pomegranates were known as 'the Crown Jewels' in the ancient Mediterranean region as they were the fruit of choice for kings and nobles. They date back to 3000 BCE and were one of the first domesticated crops in Mesopotamia, now a region of modern Iraq. They are also known for their medicinal powers — the Babylonians believed that chewing the seeds made them invincible in battle.

slightly
+(V) +(P) −(K)

Crunchy Spinach Salad

This is a delicious salad with lots of crunchy textures, colours, and flavours. Spinach is cooling, soothing, nourishing, and full of iron. It has the pungent taste essential in Ayurveda.

5-6 cups spinach leaves, chopped
½ cup red bell peppers, diced
½ cup yellow bell peppers, diced
1 cup carrots, grated
1-2 tbsp raisins or dried cranberries
2 tbsp walnuts, chopped
2 tbsp feta cheese, crumbled (optional)

Dressing:
⅓ cup olive oil
¼ cup balsamic vinegar
1 tbsp honey
1 tsp mustard
- *To reduce Pitta: omit*

Salt and freshly ground pepper to taste
1 tsp dried basil or oregano
1 clove garlic, minced (optional)
- *To reduce Pitta: omit*

In a large bowl, combine all salad ingredients and toss. In a jar, combine all dressing ingredients and shake well. Before adding dried herbs to salads, crush them between the palms of your hands to bring out the flavour. Pour over salad, toss again, and serve.

Makes **4-6 servings.**

–(V) +(P) –(K)

Cracked Wheat with Olives & Walnuts

1½ cups cracked wheat (bulgur wheat)
3 cups boiling water
½ cup parsley, chopped
⅓ cup green onions, chopped
½ cup mint leaves, chopped
1 cup tomatoes, diced
- *To reduce Pitta: use red bell peppers instead*

½ cup black olives, sliced
- *To reduce Kapha: use ¼ cup*

⅓ cup walnuts, toasted
- *To reduce Kapha: use ¼ cup*

2 tbsp extra-virgin olive oil
- *To reduce Kapha: use a light version*

4 tbsp lemon juice
1 clove garlic, minced
- *To reduce Pitta: omit*

I love this refreshing favourite with a twist: the addition of olives and nuts. The essential oils and the protein make this recipe a yummy and complete meal for lunch.

In a large bowl, combine cracked wheat and boiling water and set aside to allow cracked wheat to soak. In another bowl, combine all remaining ingredients and mix well. Once cracked wheat has absorbed the water, about 10 minutes, add other ingredients and toss. The flavours get stronger if you let this sit for a while before serving.

Makes **6 servings.**

slightly

+Ⓥ +Ⓟ −Ⓚ

Millet with Sautéed Vegetables

I made this salad for a picnic with some friends at an oceanside park. It satisfied our ravenous appetites and was a hit amidst the crashing waves and salty air. You can serve this dish warm or cold.

1 cup millet
2 cups water
2 tbsp olive oil
½ cup onions, chopped
1 cup zucchini, finely sliced and quartered
1½ cups tomatoes, diced
¾ cup mushrooms, chopped
1 tbsp soy sauce
1 tbsp rice vinegar or lemon juice
1 tsp dried basil or 2 tbsp fresh basil, chopped

In a large pot, bring millet and water to a boil. Immediately reduce heat to a simmer and cook until done, about 15 minutes. While millet is cooking, in a large frying pan on medium-high heat, sauté onions in oil. When onions start to brown, add other vegetables, and reduce to low and cook for about 10 minutes, stirring from time to time. (If mixture starts to get dry, cover it with a lid so that it can cook in its own steam.) Add soy sauce, rice vinegar, and basil and cook for another 5 minutes. Add vegetable mixture to millet and mix well. Season to taste and serve.

Makes **6 servings.**

slightly

−(V) +(P) −(K)

Buckwheat Noodle & Mango Salad

My sister Geeta shared with me her favourite potluck dish that is always a hit. It is fast and easy to prepare, yet does not compromise on style, nutrition, or flavour.

1 red bell pepper, diced
1 raw mango, peeled and diced
3 tbsp red onions, diced
½ tsp ginger, minced
2 tbsp extra-virgin olive oil
Dash of sesame oil
2 tbsp soy sauce
2-3 tbsp rice vinegar
2 bunches buckwheat noodles
Juice of ½ a lime
3 tbsp coriander leaves, chopped
Black sesame seeds (for garnish)

In a large bowl, combine peppers, mangoes, onions, ginger, oils, soy sauce, and rice vinegar. Toss well and set aside. In a large pot of boiling water, cook noodles according to package directions. Drain and set aside to cool. (Noodles may get sticky, but when you add the oil, the strands will separate.) Once cooled, add noodles to bowl and toss well. Refrigerate for a few hours. Just before serving, add lime juice, coriander, and sesame seeds and toss well.

Makes **6 servings.**

–Ⓥ +Ⓟ +Ⓚ

Sprouted Mixed Bean Salad

I like to make this early in the morning when my beans have sprouted tails of just the right length 5-mm. While the beans cook, I prepare the other ingredients; once the salad is put together, I refrigerate it until lunch or dinner. This is always a hit at my yoga retreats and makes another great take-out lunch dish.

2 cups mixed beans, sprouted and cooked
1 cup red bell peppers, chopped
1 cup celery, chopped
¼-½ cup red onions, minced

Dressing:
⅓ cup rice vinegar
⅓ cup olive oil
1 tsp mustard
1 tsp garlic, minced
1 tsp honey
Salt and freshly ground pepper to taste

In a medium bowl, combine all salad ingredients and toss. In a jar, combine all dressing ingredients and shake well. Pour over salad and toss again. Refrigerate for at least ½ hour before serving, giving the beans time to fully absorb the flavours.

Makes **4-5 servings.**

You can experiment with your own combination of beans for this recipe. I mix black beans, kidney beans, black-eyed peas, red lentils, and brown masoor lentils.

ØⓋ ØⓅ ØⓀ

New Potato Salad

This is my favourite salad for winter picnics and barbecues when new potatoes are in season. Although this recipe is tridoshic, Kaphas should eat this salad in moderation.

10-12 new potatoes (skins on)
2 stalks celery, thinly sliced
1 shallot, minced
Salt and freshly ground pepper to taste
Dash of chili flakes (optional) or ½ tsp minced green chili
½ cup coriander leaves, chopped
2 tbsp mayonnaise
- *To reduce Kapha: use a light version*

1 tsp olive oil
- *To reduce Vata: increase to 1 tbsp*

In a large pot of salted water, bring potatoes to a boil. Reduce heat to a simmer and cook until done, 15-20 minutes. While potatoes are cooking, in a large bowl, combine celery, shallots, salt, pepper, chili flakes, and coriander and mix well. Drain potatoes and cut in halves or quarters. In a bowl, toss potatoes with olive oil and mayonnaise while still warm, then add other mixture and mix well. Serve slightly warm or chilled.

Makes **2-4 servings.**

slightly
−Ⓥ +Ⓟ +Ⓚ

Spicy French Dressing

This recipe is based on a dressing that is a mainstay in my family. It adds a rich, tangy flavour to any fresh salad. Try pairing it with one garnished with onions or coriander leaves, or drizzle it over fresh sliced tomatoes.

½ cup olive oil (or flax seed or hemp oil)
½ cup vinegar
Salt and freshly ground pepper to taste
¼ tsp cayenne pepper
½ tsp mustard
2 tsp honey or sweetener (optional)

In a jar, combine all ingredients and mix well, ensuring honey dissolves and mustard does not clump.

Makes **1 cup.**

−(V) +(P) −(K)

Fortifying Lemon & Garlic Dressing

4-6 tbsp lemon juice
4 tbsp flax seed or hemp oil
- *To reduce Kapha: use 2 tbsp or omit and add 2 tbsp more lemon juice*

1-2 tsp garlic, minced
Salt and freshly ground pepper to taste
1 tbsp fresh herbs (or ½ tsp dry) (optional)

This dressing is for garlic lovers. It is very effective for cleansing the system and fending off colds (garlic is a natural antibiotic). This is a light, refreshing dressing, especially if you reduce or omit the oil.

In a jar, combine all ingredients and shake well. For a stronger flavour, refrigerate for a minimum of 10 minutes before using.

Makes ½ **cup.**

Variations:
- *Olive Oil & Vinegar Dressing:* ½ cup olive oil, ⅓ cup balsamic vinegar, salt and freshly ground pepper to taste. In a jar, combine all ingredients and shake well.
- *Tridoshic Salad Dressing:* 1 tbsp light olive oil, ¼ cup rice vinegar, salt and freshly ground pepper to taste. In a jar, combine all ingredients and shake well.

slightly
−Ⓥ +Ⓟ −Ⓚ

Thai Salad Dressing

I love this dressing's mixture of the sweet and sour flavours. Sesame oil is full of healing and detoxifying properties that benefit the brain and nervous system. This is a wonderful pick-me-up if you are feeling sedentary (for Kapha states) and has the sweet and sour tastes to calm Vata. To give the dressing more kick, add the suggested garnishes to your favourite salad.

Dressing:

1 tbsp ginger, grated or finely chopped
1 tsp garlic, minced
- *To reduce Pitta: omit*

4 tbsp lime juice
4 tbsp olive oil
- *To reduce Kapha: use a light version*

Dash of sesame oil
1 tbsp or soy sauce
1 tbsp honey

Salad garnishes:

½ tsp green chilies, minced, or to taste
- *To reduce Pitta: omit*

¼ cup coriander leaves, chopped
¼ cup basil leaves, chopped

In a jar, combine all dressing ingredients and shake well. Add garnishes to salad and toss. Pour dressing over salad, toss again, and serve.

Makes **½ cup dressing.**

slightly
−(V) +(P) −(K)

Creamy Coriander Dressing

This lovely and light dressing is delicious on your favourite salads and on sliced cucumbers, and its combination of spices makes it good for all *doshas*.

½ cup plain yogurt
- *To reduce Kapha: use light yogurt*

¼ tsp turmeric
2 tbsp lemon juice
¼ tsp ground coriander
⅛ tsp ground cardamom
½ tsp sugar syrup
- *To reduce Kapha: use honey*

½ tsp ginger, minced
1 clove garlic, crushed or minced
Salt and freshly ground pepper to taste
¼ tsp green chilies, minced
- *To reduce Pitta: omit*

¼ cup coriander leaves, finely chopped

In a bowl, combine all ingredients and mix together well.

Makes **½ cup.**

–Ⓥ –Ⓟ –Ⓚ
Ⓓ

Tofu with Green Onions

My cousin Ameeta, is also a yoga instructor and has been a vegetarian for ages. On my last visit, she prepared a wonderful dinner for me, which included this dish that I now frequently make at my yoga retreats.

1½ cups tofu
1 cup coriander leaves, chopped
½ cup green onions, sliced
2 tbsp sesame seeds
¼ tsp dried red chili flakes (optional)
- *To reduce Pitta: omit*

Dressing:
¼ cup soy sauce
2 tbsp ginger, grated
1 tbsp sesame seed oil
1 tsp mustard
¼ cup lemon juice

Drain tofu, wrap in a dish towel, and set aside to dry. Meanwhile, in a jar, combine all dressing ingredients, shake well to mix, and set aside. Slice tofu into 1½-cm thick slices and place in a medium bowl. Pour dressing over tofu to marinate for at least 30 minutes. Add coriander leaves, green onions, sesame seeds, and chili flakes (if using). Toss and serve.

Makes **4-6 servings.**

Ingredients such as ginger, soy, chili, and mustard warm the cool tofu and aid its digestion. Lemon juice stimulates the digestive fire (agni) and coriander balances all the doshas. Eating tofu in excess will imbalance Kapha.

–Ⓥ +Ⓟ –Ⓚ

The Dainty Cachumber

This is one of my favourite salads that gives depth to any meal. Tomatoes are a rich source of vitamins A and C. Vatas and Pittas only need a small portion whereas Kaphas can indulge.

1 onion, sliced
2 large tomatoes, cubed
3 tbsp apple cider or rice vinegar
¼ tsp salt
¼ tsp cayenne pepper or fresh green chilies, chopped (optional)
¼ cup coriander leaves, minced (optional)

In a large bowl, combine all ingredients, toss, and serve. Refrigerate the salad for ½ hour to enhance the flavours.

Makes **4-6 servings.**

Soups are comfort food; they also make nourishing appetizers and snacks, and some are hearty enough to be complete meals in themselves. Soups replenish us when we are tired or run down, quickly and efficiently filling our need for essential nutrients without taxing the digestive system. In particular, clear soups calm the nervous system, while other light soups cleanse our digestive tracts if we have consumed too many heavy foods. Soups also are a great way to use any odds and ends in the refrigerator and pantry for a delicious, spur-of-the-moment meal. (Having said that, keep in mind that the fresher your ingredients, the better the soup!) Adding beans, lentils, tofu, or miso gives soups the protein content we all need.

Soups

This section includes both lighter and heartier recipes. *The Clear Vegetable Soup* (page 94) can be nourishing either on its own or as a base for other soups. *The Sprouted Mung Bean Soup* (page 99) is filled with protein, vitamins, minerals, and essential amino acids — the building blocks to good health which benefit all constitutions. *The Beat the Cold Soup* (page 98) really works when you are feeling under the weather. And the chickpea and lentil soups are substantial meals when paired with your favourite bread.

slightly
−Ⓥ +Ⓟ −Ⓚ

Clear Vegetable Soup

This is a fragrant consommé that can be enjoyed on its own or as a stock for your favourite soup recipe.

1 cup onions, roughly chopped
1¼ cups carrots, roughly chopped
1¼ cups celery, roughly chopped
⅓ cup coriander leaves, roughly chopped
1¼ cup apples, roughly chopped
3 slices ginger (optional)
2 bay leaves
10 whole peppercorns
- *To reduce Pitta: use 4*

1 cinnamon stick (about 5-cm long)
2 cloves
- *To reduce Pitta: omit*

Salt to taste
¼ tsp turmeric
¼ cup fresh herbs
10 cups water

In a large pot on high heat, combine all ingredients and bring to a boil. Immediately reduce heat to a simmer, cover with lid, and cook for 45 minutes. Strain before serving or using.

Makes **8-10 cups.**

Variations:

- Add 3 whole garlic cloves; juice of ½ a lemon (To reduce Kapha: omit); and 1 cup parsley, roughly chopped.
- Omit cinnamon stick, ginger, and coriander leaves.

–Ⓥ +Ⓟ –Ⓚ

Carrot Ginger Soup

I love this soup's sweet taste from the caramelized onions and carrots combined with warm spices. Carrots are a rich source of vitamin A and ginger is good for the circulation and digestion.

1½ tbsp olive oil
2 cups onions, chopped
4 tsp ginger, minced
- *To reduce Pitta: use 1 tsp ginger*

7 cups carrots, chopped
- *To reduce Pitta: use 5 cups carrots and 2 cups celery*

5 cups water
2 tsp salt
1 cinnamon stick (about 5-cm long)
10 whole peppercorns
- *To reduce Pitta: use 5 whole peppercorns*

2 tbsp parsley, chopped (for garnish)

In a medium pot on medium-low, heat oil. Add onions and ginger and sauté until onions are caramelized, about 5-8 minutes. Stir in carrots, water, salt, cinnamon stick, and peppercorns. Bring to a boil, cover, then reduce heat to simmer until done, about 15-20 minutes. Remove cinnamon stick and peppercorns. In a blender or food processor, purée until smooth. (Be careful when blending hot liquids.) Garnish with parsley and serve.

Makes **6-8 cups.**

Whole peppercorns add flavour without a lot of heat. If you don't purée them, be sure to remove them before serving to avoid biting into one.

slightly slightly
−Ⓥ +Ⓟ +Ⓚ

Spiced Pumpkin Soup

This warm and nourishing soup is great anytime of the year.

- 2 tsp good oil (page 27)
- 1 medium onion, chopped
- 1 clove garlic, minced
- ½ tsp ginger, grated
- ½ tsp ground cumin
- 1 green chili, slit at end (optional)
  - *To reduce Pitta: use ¼ green chili, slit*
- 4 cups vegetable stock (page 94)
- 4 cups pumpkin, cubed
- 1 tsp sugar syrup (optional)
- ¼ tsp ground nutmeg (for garnish)
- 2 tbsp coriander leaves, chopped (or parsley) (for garnish)

In a large pot on medium-low, heat oil. Add onions and sauté for about 4 minutes. Stir in garlic, ginger, cumin, and green chili and continue to sauté until onions are caramelized, about 4 minutes. Add vegetable stock and pumpkin. Cook until pumpkin is soft, about 10-15 minutes, then stir in sugar syrup. In a blender or food processor, purée until smooth. (Be careful when blending hot liquids.) Garnish with nutmeg and coriander and serve.

Makes **4-6 cups.**

-Ⓥ -Ⓟ -Ⓚ
Ⓓ

Spinach Vegetable Soup

This recipe offers a tasty, easy way to get a hearty serving of vegetables and nutrients.

1 tbsp olive oil
1 cup onions, sliced
½ tsp ginger, minced
½ tsp ground cumin
2 cups water
2 cups of vegetable stock (page 94)
1 cup sweet potatoes, cubed
½ cup carrots, sliced
5-6 cups spinach, chopped
Salt and freshly ground pepper to taste

In a large pot on medium-high, heat oil. Add onions and ginger and sauté until onions start to caramelize, about 5 minutes. Stir in cumin and sauté for another minute. Add water, vegetable stock, and all vegetables. Cook until sweet potatoes are softened, about 15 minutes. Stir in salt and pepper, then serve.

Makes **4-6 cups.**

−Ⓥ +Ⓟ −Ⓚ

Beat the Cold Soup

I live in rainy part of the country where residents seem to suffer from colds at least twice a year. The last time I started to feel a cold setting in, I created this soup to 'beat' it!

1 tbsp good oil (page 27)
½ cup onions, chopped
3 tsp ginger, minced
2 tsp green chilies, minced
  • *To reduce Pitta: omit*
2 tsp garlic, minced
½ cup celery, diced
½ cup carrots, diced
¼ tsp cayenne pepper
½ tsp turmeric
½ tsp garam masala
½ cup mushrooms, chopped
¾ cup zucchini, chopped
¼ cup tomatoes, diced
2 cups vegetable stock (page 94)
4 whole peppercorns
2 cloves
1 cup broccoli and cauliflower florets (mixed),
Juice of 1 lemon
Salt to taste
¼ cup coriander leaves, chopped (for garnish)

In a large pot on medium-high, heat oil. Add onions, ginger, and green chilies and sauté until onions start to soften, about 4 minutes. Stir in garlic and celery and continue to sauté for a few minutes. Add carrots, cayenne, turmeric, and garam masala and sauté for a few more minutes. Add mushrooms and zucchini and sauté for another minute. Stir in tomatoes and sauté for an additional minute. Add vegetable stock, peppercorns, and cloves, then reduce heat and simmer for 10 minutes. Add broccoli and cauliflower florets and cook for another 7 minutes until softened. Just before soup is done, stir in lemon juice and salt to taste. Remove peppercorns, garnish with coriander and serve.

Makes **4-6 cups.**

–Ⓥ –Ⓟ –Ⓚ
Ⓓ

Sprouted Mung Bean Soup

Sprouted mung beans are filled with protein and amino acids, which are the building blocks to good health. This soup is balancing and restorative for all the doshas, and easy to digest. If you use cooked mung beans instead of sprouted, your soup will be ready after only 5 minutes of simmering.

1 tbsp olive oil
- *To reduce Kapha: use a light version*

¼ cup onions, chopped
1 tsp fresh ginger, minced
1 tsp fresh green chilies, minced
- *To reduce Pitta: only use half the amount or omit*

¼ cup celery, chopped
4 cups vegetable stock (page 94)
3 cups sprouted mung beans (page 30)
Juice of ½ a lime

In a large pot on medium, heat oil. Add onions, ginger, and green chilies and sauté for 1 minute. Add celery and continue to sauté for 5-6 minutes, until onions are caramelized. Add vegetable stock and sprouted mung beans. Bring to a boil, then immediately reduce heat to low and simmer until done, 20-30 minutes. Stir in lime juice and serve.

Makes **4-6 servings.**

Variations:
- Add these just before serving: 6 tbsp plain yogurt (to reduce Kapha: use a light version) 6 tsp *Tamarind Chutney* (page 174); ¼ cup fresh coriander leaves, chopped.
- Add 6 tsp *Coriander Garlic Chutney* (page 173) just before serving.

–Ⓥ –Ⓟ –Ⓚ

Asparagus Miso Soup

This soup is great for your body — miso is a good source of protein that is smooth and easy to digest, and asparagus calms the nervous system.

1 tsp olive oil
¼ cup onions, chopped
1 tsp ginger, minced
6 cups vegetable stock
3 cups hot water
2 cups sweet potatoes, diced
- *To reduce Kapha: use regular potatoes*

2 cups asparagus, chopped
Freshly ground pepper to taste
A pinch of cayenne pepper (optional)
Squeeze of lemon juice
1 tbsp miso paste
Salt or soy sauce to taste
1 tbsp plain yogurt (or sour cream) (for garnish)

In a large pot on medium-high, heat oil. Add onions and ginger and sauté until onions start to soften, about 4 minutes. Add vegetable stock, sweet potatoes and bring to a boil. Reduce heat and simmer for 10 minutes. Add asparagus and cook for an additional 5-10 minutes, until vegetables are just softened. Add pepper, cayenne, lemon juice, and miso, and stir continually until miso dissolves completely. Check for seasoning. Add salt or soy sauce, if necessary; if soup is too salty, add a little water. Remove from heat and lightly mash soup, leaving it somewhat chunky; if you prefer a thinner soup, add a bit more water. Garnish with yogurt (or sour cream) and serve.

Makes **4 cups.**

slightly
−(V) +(P) −(K)

Miso Soup with Tofu & Seaweed

This is a great energy booster to serve as a starter, snack, or meal; as easy to make as a cup of tea! You can presoak the seaweed in cold water for 15 minutes before adding it to the soup, but I prefer simply boiling it with the water and watching it come to life! It should double in size when ready.

4½ cups water
1 tbsp thin black seaweed
4 tbsp miso paste
¼ cup tofu, cubed
2 green onions, white parts only, chopped
A dash of cayenne pepper

In a large pot on high heat, combine water and seaweed. Bring to a boil, then turn off heat. Add miso and stir until dissolved completely. Stir in tofu, onions, and cayenne and serve.

Makes **4 cups.**

slightly

−Ⓥ +Ⓟ −Ⓚ

Hearty Red Lentil & Vegetable Soup

A wonderful one-dish meal, packed with nutrients and protein.

2 tsp olive oil
½ cup onions, chopped
1½ tsp garlic, minced
1 tsp ginger, minced
- *To reduce Pitta: omit*

½ cup celery, diced
½ tsp ground coriander
½ tsp ground cumin
¼ tsp cayenne pepper
½ tsp turmeric
1 cup carrots, sliced
¾ cup tomatoes chopped
¼ cup parsley, chopped
2 bay leaves
1 tsp salt, or to taste
4 whole peppercorns
3 cloves
4 cups water
¼ cup barley
½ cup red lentils

In a large pot on medium-high, heat oil. Add onions, garlic, ginger, and celery and sauté for a minute. Stir in coriander, cumin, cayenne, and turmeric and sauté for another 2 minutes. Add carrots and sauté for 2-3 minutes. When liquid in mixture starts to evaporate, add tomatoes. Cook for another few minutes. Add parsley, bay leaves, salt, peppercorns, cloves, water, and barley, reduce heat to medium, and cook for 20 minutes. If you are pressed for time, omit the barley, add lentils with the water, and cook for another 20 minutes until lentils are soft. Stir in lentils, reduce heat to simmer, and cook for 25 minutes until lentils are soft. Remove bay leaves and peppercorns, and serve.

Makes **4-6 cups.**

slightly

+(V) −(P) +(K)

Spicy Chickpea Soup with Coconut

Serve this filling soup with fresh bread for a complete meal.

- 1½ tbsp good oil (page 27) (for onions)
- ¾ cup onions, chopped
- 1½ tbsp good oil (for mustard seeds)
- 1 tsp black mustard seeds
- 1 tsp garlic, minced
- • To reduce Pitta: omit
- 1 tsp ginger, minced
- 1 tsp turmeric
- 2 tsp ground coriander (or cumin)
- 2 cups chickpeas cooked (page 31)
- 3 cups vegetable stock (page 94)
- 6 curry leaves
- ½ cup coconut milk
- 2 tbsp *Tamarind Chutney* (page 174) (or 2 tbsp lemon juice and 1 tsp maple syrup)
- ½ cup coriander leaves, chopped (for garnish)
- ½ cup plain yogurt (for garnish)

In a large pot on medium-low, heat 1½ tbsp oil. Add onions and sauté until caramelized, about 6-8 minutes. Push onions to one side of pot and heat another 1½ tbsp oil. Add mustard seeds, cover with lid, and let pop for 30 seconds, then stir together with onions. Add garlic, ginger, turmeric, coriander (or cumin), and sauté for another 3-4 minutes. Add chickpeas and stir for another few minutes. Add vegetable stock and curry leaves and simmer for 15-20 minutes. Discard curry leaves.

Pour half the mixture from pot into a blender or food processor. Add coconut milk and purée until smooth, then return to the pot. (Be careful when blending hot liquids.) Add tamarind chutney and stir well. In a separate bowl, combine coriander leaves and yogurt. Garnish soup with a dollop of coriander-yogurt mixture, and serve.

Makes **4-6 cups.**

Curry leaves are used in soups for their distinct flavour and healing properties. In Ayurveda, they are known to be detoxifying, cooling, and bitter.

–(V) –(P) +(K)

Chilled Cucumber & Coconut Soup

This is a refreshing, cooling soup with a perfect mixture of warming spices.

2 cups cucumbers, chopped
½ tsp salt, or to taste
2 cloves garlic
- *To reduce Pitta: omit*

1 tsp ginger, minced
¼ cup mint leaves, chopped
½ cup coriander leaves, chopped
1 tsp green chilies, minced
- *To reduce Pitta: omit*

Juice of 1 lime
¼ tsp ground cumin
1 cup coconut, grated
2 cups plain yogurt
¼ cup coriander leaves, chopped (for garnish)
¼ tsp cayenne pepper (for garnish)

In a bowl, combine cucumbers, salt, garlic, ginger, mint, coriander leaves, chilies, lime juice, and cumin and mix well. Cover and refrigerate for 3-4 hours. Once chilled, in a food processor or a blender, purée mixture and coconut. Pour into a serving dish, and stir in yogurt until smooth. If too thick, add ¼ cup of water. Garnish with coriander leaves, sprinkle with cayenne, and serve.

Makes **4 cups.**

+Ⓥ +Ⓟ −Ⓚ

Kathy's Gazpacho

It was through Kathy that I first discovered Bowen Island, where I now reside and where cooking and sharing meals is celebrated. Every summer, when Kathy spends time on Bowen Island, her refrigerator is never without this soup. It is refreshing and light and has all the nourishment needed on hot sunny days.

2 cloves garlic
1 large jalapeño pepper
2 cups cucumbers, roughly chopped
2 celery stalks with leaves, sliced
1 red bell pepper, roughly chopped
1 small red onion, sliced
4 tomatoes, sliced
1 avocado, roughly chopped
1 cup parsley, roughly chopped
1 cup tomato juice
½ cup lime juice
¼ cup flax seed or hemp oil
1 tsp ground cumin
Salt and freshly ground pepper to taste
A few parsley sprigs (for garnish)
1 cup plain yogurt (for garnish)

- *To reduce Kapha: omit or use a light version*

In a blender or food processor, mince garlic and jalapeño. Add cucumbers, celery, red bell peppers, onions, and tomatoes and pulse. Add remaining ingredients except garnishes, and pulse until quite smooth. Refrigerate until chilled. Garnish with a dollop of yogurt and a sprig of parsley, then serve.

Makes **6-8 cups.**

–Ⓥ –Ⓟ –Ⓚ Ⓓ

Chilled Mixed Fruit Soup

My friend Kathy has wonderful dinner parties in the summer and often serves this as the starter, making it a great conversation piece. Fresh fruit is always best eaten on its own, or 15 minutes before another course — it's good for the digestion.

3 cups strawberries, quartered
3 nectarines, pitted and diced
3 plums, pitted and chopped
2½ cups blueberries
1 cup raspberries
1 cup blackberries
1½ cups peach juice
- *To reduce Vata: use fresh orange juice*

3 cups water
6 tbsp sweetener
½ tsp cinnamon
1½ cups plain yogurt (for garnish)
- *To reduce Pitta and Kapha: use a light version*

Sprigs of fresh mint (for garnish)

In a large bowl, combine ½ cup of strawberries, 1 nectarine, 1 cup of blueberries, and all the raspberries and blackberries and set aside. In a large pot, combine all remaining ingredients except garnishes and bring to a boil. Reduce heat to low and simmer until fruit is soft, about 15 minutes. In a blender or food processor, purée until smooth. (Be careful when blending hot liquids.) Return to pot, add reserved fruit while soup is still hot. Let cool, then cover with lid and refrigerate until chilled, about 30 minutes. Garnish with a dollop of yogurt and some mint leaves, then serve.

Makes **10 servings.**

In Indian cooking, a meal rarely consists of a single dish; traditionally, several dishes are served in combination. A complete 'entrée' includes a protein (e.g., beans or tofu), a grain (e.g., rice or chapatis), vegetables, raita and pickles, and something raw to aid digestion (e.g., salad). An ideal meal includes all six tastes — sweet, sour, salty, pungent, bitter, and astringent — to balance out the *doshas* (page 21).

It is important to eat meals that suit your constitution and state of *agni* or digestive fire. If your *agni* is low — you feel heavy or lethargic after eating — choose meals that will gently restore it

Entrées

(e.g., *the khichari* or *mung dal* with simple spices). Eating meals that are too heavy for an overtaxed digestive system can be compared to putting too much wood on a small fire: it will be smothered and go out. If your agni is treated correctly with proper food choices and portions, its fire should easily consume or 'digest' the food, giving you constant energy and a balanced feeling, sustaining you until your next meal.

Our bodies are most familiar with foods we eat in our own particular 'culture,' so when you introduce new foods into your diet, start slowly to allow your body to assimilate them. Remember, your body speaks to you, telling you what it needs; listen to it.

This section begins with the essential three elements of a nutritious and balanced Ayurvedic meal. First are bean, lentil, and tofu dishes that I call 'the meat' of the book. The rice dishes follow because when combined with legumes, they create a complete protein. Next are the vegetable dishes, filled with flavour and nutrients, then *Spiced 'Buttermilk' Curry* (page 147). You can mix-and-match protein, rice, and vegetable dishes to create a nutritionally-balanced meal that suits your own particular *dosha*.

Beans, Lentils & Tofu

Pulses or legumes mixed with grains are a staple of many diets all over the world and are an essential component of eating the Ayurvedic way to maintain health and vitality. The combination of pulses with grains (usually rice), which add the essential amino acids that pulses lack, forms a complete protein. The most beneficial serving ratio of rice to pulses for optimal complete protein content is about 2:1; e.g., 1 cup of rice to half cup of lentils.

Incorporating more beans and lentils (along with rice or other grains) into your meals is a great way to improve your health as they are known to decrease blood fats and hardening of the arteries, lower cholesterol levels, and promote a healthy heart. Pulses are a good source of iron and B vitamins and are high in fiber and low in fat. Some people find beans and lentils difficult to digest; those who do, or those who do not already eat them regularly, should introduce them into their diet slowly (about once or twice a week) to give the digestive tract time to adapt.

Before cooking, it is best to soak dried beans and lentils overnight as it helps to break down the starches and their notorious gassy properties — some pulses do not require soaking. Plus, soaking shortens the cooking time while increasing their protein and vitamin C content. Pre-soaking, or 'sprouting,' pulses also increases their nutritional value (up to an amazing forty times!) as it is brings the seed that was dormant back to life.

After soaking, beans and lentils must be cooked thoroughly to ensure easy digestion. You'll know they are done when they are tender in the middle without being mushy — with the exception of *mung bean* and *masoor*, which inevitably turn mushy and somewhat soupy.

Mung beans are among the easiest to digest, making them beneficial for all the *doshas*. They are considered cooling and restorative, giving strength and vitality. The cooling qualities of *mung beans* are best balanced by warm spices — like ginger, green chilies, cumin, and mustard seeds — to aid digestion. Additionally, the sour tastes of lemon or *Tamarind Chutney* (page 174) will further help to stimulate *agni*. Rajma and chana are more difficult to digest and should only be eaten when *agni* is high, a common attribute of Pitta. If you want to calm excess Vata, look for recipes with *urad dal*. Kaphas will benefit from the dishes *Chickpea Curry* (page 111), *Quick & Easy Red Masoor Dal* (page 121), and *Strengthening Tur Dal* (page 118).

Type of Beans	Amount of Water for Soaking	Soaking Time	Cooking time	Yields Amount of Cooked Beans
All Beans	2-3 cups	6-8 hours	40-60 min (dependent on soaking time)	2 cups
Azuki beans	"	"	"	3 cups
Black beans	"	"	"	2¼ cups
Kidney beans	"	"	"	2¼ cups
Red, brown, and green dal	Not required	Not required	20 min	2½ cups
Split yellow mung beans	Not required	Not required	20 min	2 cups
Tur dal	2-3 cups	1-2 hours	40-60 min (dependent on soaking time)	2 cups

* Amount of beans is 1 cup. ** 3-4 cups of water for cooking.

slightly

−(V) −(P) +(K)

Kala Chana in Coconut Sauce

1 cup black chickpeas
1 tbsp good oil (page 27)
1 tsp mustard seeds
2 cups tomatoes, diced
1 tsp ginger
1 clove garlic, minced
½ tsp ground cumin
½ tsp ground coriander
¼ tsp cayenne pepper
¼ tsp turmeric
Salt to taste
¾ cup coconut milk
- *To reduce Kapha: use a light version*

4-5 curry leaves
Juice of 1 lemon (or Tamarind Chutney, page 174)
1 cup onions, thinly sliced
1 tsp *ghee* (or butter)
1 tsp olive oil

Black chickpeas (*kala chana*), are smaller in size than white. They have an earthy taste and a robust, nutty flavour, and the combination of spices, caramelized onions, and coconut sauce gives this dish its rich flavour. It is good served with rice.

Soak and cook chickpeas (page 31). In a large pot on medium-high, heat oil. Add mustard seeds, cover with lid, and let pop for 30 seconds. Immediately add tomatoes, ginger, garlic, cumin, coriander, cayenne, turmeric, and salt. Reduce heat to medium and sauté until tomatoes have softened and spices are cooked, about 8-10 minutes. Add cooked chickpeas, coconut milk, and curry leaves. Cook for another 10-15 minutes. Add lemon juice, stir, and remove from heat. (If dish is too thick or too salty, add more water.) In a frying pan on medium, heat *ghee* and olive oil. Add onions and sauté until caramelized, about 8-10 minutes. Add to chickpea mixture, remove curry leaves, and serve.

Makes **4 servings.**

To make your own 'light' coconut milk, simply add water to it, i.e. half regular coconut milk to half water.

+(V) −(P) −(K)

Chickpea Curry

Chickpea (*kabuli chana*) curry is best served with rice or chapatis and a *Raita*; add green vegetables and the *Dainty Cachumber* (page 92), and you have a complete meal!

1⅔ cups chickpeas
1½ cups reserved water
2 tbsp good oil (page 27)
¼ cup onions, minced
1 tbsp ginger, minced
¼ tsp turmeric
½ tsp ground cumin
½ tsp ground coriander
½ tsp garam masala
¼ cayenne pepper, or to taste
Juice of 1 lemon
¼ cup coriander leaves, chopped (for garnish)

Soak and cook chickpeas until they are done (page 31). Save 1½ cups of water that the chickpeas were cooked in to add to this recipe. In a medium pot on medium, heat oil. Add onions and sauté until they start to brown, 3-4 minutes. Add ginger, turmeric, cumin, coriander, garam masala, and cayenne, and sauté for another minute. Add chickpeas and reserved water. Bring liquid to a boil, then reduce heat to medium and simmer for about 20 minutes. When chickpeas are tender but not mushy, add lemon juice and adjust for salt. Serve garnished with coriander.

Makes **4-6 servings.**

slightly slightly
+(V) +(P) −(K)

Masala Patties (or Dokri Nu Shak)

Filled with protein and calcium, these spicy patties are worth the few steps it takes to make them. It is hard not to start eating these after covering them with the masala sauce, but if you can wait and let the spices intensify for an hour or two, it's worth it! The secret to this recipe is sifting the flour to avoid lumps and using a metal whisk.

Patties:
2 cups gram flour
¾ cup onions, chopped
2-3 green chilies, chopped
- *To reduce Pitta: use less or omit*

¾ tsp ground cumin
¾ tsp ground coriander
1½ tsp salt
Juice of 1 lemon or lime

Masala:
¼ cup grapeseed oil (or good oil, page 27)
1 tsp black mustard seeds
½ tsp whole cumin seeds
2 dried red chilies
- *To reduce Pitta: use 1*

6-8 curry leaves (optional)
2 cups tomatoes, diced
1 tsp ginger, minced
1 clove garlic, minced
- *To reduce Pitta: omit*

¾ tsp ground cumin
¾ tsp ground coriander
¼ tsp turmeric
1½ tsp salt
Juice of 1 lemon
1 tbsp tomato paste

For the patties:
In a medium bowl, sift flour, then add all remaining patty ingredients, mix well, and set aside. In a large pot, bring 4 cups of water to a boil. Add patty mixture then reduce heat to low. Stir continuously with a whisk to avoid lumps, and cook for 10-15 minutes until it begins to bubble. On a lightly greased baking sheet, spread the cooked mixture with a spatula to make a (30 x 30-cm) square and let it cool. When it has completely cooled, cut into 4-cm squares and separate.

For the masala:
In a large frying pan on medium-high, heat oil. Add mustard seeds, cumin seeds, chilies, and curry leaves. Cover with lid for 30 seconds while the mustard

2 cups plain yogurt
½ cup water
1 tbsp gram flour
¼ cup coriander leaves, chopped (for garnish)

seeds pop. Stir in remaining masala ingredients except yogurt, water, flour, and coriander leaves. Reduce heat to medium-low and cook for 15-20 minutes, until oil appears on the surface. Gently add the square patties to the masala and cover them with sauce. Turn off heat.

Just before serving, in a bowl, beat together yogurt, water, and gram flour, ensuring there are no lumps. Add to the masala and patties and heat on low for about 5 minutes until heated through. (Do not overcook as the patties will absorb too much liquid.) Garnish with fresh coriander leaves and serve. Serve immediately or let sit for 1-2 hours for flavours to intensify.

Makes **4-6 servings.**

+(V) −(P) −(K)

Quick Black Beans

I like making this when I'm hungry and want a tasty, satisfying meal. The leftovers are great for lunch the next day. Serve with rice or your favourite bread.

1 tbsp good oil (page 27)
1 tsp sesame oil
¾ cup onions, chopped
½ tsp ginger, minced
1 tsp garlic, minced (about 1 clove)
- *To reduce Pitta: omit*

½ tsp green chilies, chopped
- *To reduce Pitta: omit*

1 cup zucchini, quartered and sliced
1 cup yellow bell peppers, diced
1 cup red bell peppers, diced
2 cups spinach
Tamari (or salt) to taste
Chili sauce to taste
- *To reduce Pitta: omit*

2 cups black beans, cooked (page 31)
½ cup plain yogurt (for garnish)
¼ cup coriander leaves, chopped (for garnish)

In a pot on medium-high, heat oils. Add onions, ginger, garlic, and chilies, and sauté for 1-2 minutes. Add zucchini, peppers, spinach, tamari (or salt), and chili sauce. Cover with lid, reduce heat to medium, and cook for 4-5 minutes. Add beans and mix until heated through. Serve in individual bowls with a dollop of yogurt and a sprinkling of coriander.

Makes **2 servings.**

slightly
+Ⓥ –Ⓟ øⓀ

Small Red Bean Curry

2 cups small red beans
2 tbsp good oil (page 27)
1 cup onions, minced
2 tbsp ginger, minced
2 tsp garlic, minced
2 tsp ground coriander
1 tsp ground cumin
1 tsp garam masala
1½ cups tomatoes, cubed
Juice of 1 lemon
3 tbsp coriander leaves, chopped (for garnish)

I took this to a potluck dinner and it was polished off with rave reviews! Small red beans are smaller, slightly rounder, and darker versions of red kidney beans. You can substitute red kidney beans for small red beans. Coriander leaves balances all the *doshas*. Serve this with rice or chapatis, *Cumin Raita* (page 182), and a vegetable dish for a complete, balanced meal.

Soak and cook red beans until they are ⅔ done (page 31). In a frying pan on medium-high, heat oil. Add onions, ginger, and garlic, reduce heat to medium and sauté until onions are caramelized, about 5-6 minutes. Add coriander, cumin, and garam masala and sauté for another 30 seconds. Stir in tomatoes and cook for about 5 minutes until tomatoes turn soft. Add mixture to cooked beans and cook for 15-20 minutes until beans are cooked through. Add lemon juice and adjust for salt. Garnish with coriander leaves and serve.

Makes **6 servings.**

−(V) −(P) −(K)

Balancing Mung Dal (D)

Split yellow mung dal cooks quickly and balances all three *doshas*. It is nourishing and easy on the digestive system.

2 cups split yellow mung dal
5-6 cups water
1 green chili, slit at end
- *To reduce Pitta: use ¼ or omit*

1 2½-cm piece ginger, sliced
2 tsp salt
¼ tsp turmeric
1 tsp olive oil

Tadka:

1 tbsp olive oil (I use half *ghee* and half olive oil)
1 tsp whole cumin seeds
¾ cup onions, sliced
1 tbsp ginger, minced
1 tsp salt, or to taste
1 green chili, minced
- *To reduce Pitta: use ¼ or omit*

¼ cup coriander leaves, chopped (for garnish)
1 tomato, sliced (for garnish)
- *To reduce Pitta: omit*

In a large pot, combine all dal ingredients and bring to a boil. Reduce heat to medium and simmer until done, about 20-25 minutes.

In a frying pan on medium-high, heat oil. Add cumin seeds and let sizzle for about 10 seconds. Add remaining tadka ingredients. Reduce heat to medium and sauté until onions are caramelized, about 7-8 minutes.

To serve, place cooked dal in a serving dish. Spread tadka on top and garnish with coriander leaves and tomato slices.

Makes **4-6 servings.**

–Ⓥ –Ⓟ –Ⓚ
Ⓓ

The King Dal

Whole mung dal is considered the 'king' of beans and lentils because of its amino-acid content that balances and nourishes all the *doshas*.

½ cup whole green mung dal
3 cups water (for soaking)
1 tbsp good oil (page 27)
¼ tsp mustard seeds
⅛ tsp asafoetida
2 cups water
¼ tsp turmeric
¼ tsp cayenne pepper (optional)
- *To reduce Pitta: omit*

Salt to taste
Juice of ½ a lemon
1 tbsp coriander leaves (or parsley), chopped (for garnish)

Soak mung dal in 3 cups water for at least 4 hours or overnight. Drain and set aside. In a medium pot on medium-high, heat oil. Add mustard seeds, cover with lid, and let pop about 30 seconds. Immediately add soaked dal, asafoetida, water, turmeric, cayenne, and salt. Bring to a boil, then reduce heat to simmer until done, about 40-60 minutes. (The longer the dal has soaked, the less water it needs and time to cook.) Check from time to time in case you need to add more water. Add lemon juice, garnish with coriander leaves, and serve.

Makes **3-4 servings.**

−Ⓥ +Ⓟ −Ⓚ

Strengthening Tur Dal

Tur or arhar is a blood builder and strengthens muscles; it is also good for bones, joints, skin, and eyes. to make this dal a one-pot meal add chopped carrots and quartered potatoes to cook with the dal.

2 cups tur dal
6 cups water (for soaking)
7 cups water (for cooking)
1 tsp salt
⅛ tsp asafoetida
¼ tsp turmeric
1 tsp good oil
4-6 curry leaves (optional)

Tadka:
2 tsp good oil (page 27)
2-3 dried red chilies
1 tsp black mustard seeds
1 tsp ginger, minced
1 tsp garlic, minced
1 tsp salt
½ tsp turmeric
1 tsp ground cumin
1 tsp ground coriander
¼ tsp cayenne pepper, or to taste
- *To reduce Pitta: omit*

1 cup tomatoes, chopped
2 tbsp tomato purée
2 tbsp lemon juice
1 tsp sweetener (optional)
¼ cup coriander leaves, chopped (for garnish)

Soak dal in 6 cups water for 1-2 hours. Drain before using. In a large pot on high heat, combine 7 cups water and tur dal and bring to a boil. Skim off froth with a slotted spoon. Add turmeric, salt, asafoetida, oil, and curry leaves (if using). Reduce heat and simmer for 45 minutes.

While the dal cooks, in a frying pan on medium-high, heat oil. Add chilies and sauté until they turn black. Immediately add mustard seeds, cover with a lid, and let pop for 30 seconds. Immediately add remaining tadka ingredients, except lemon juice and sweetener, and sauté until oil appears on the surface, about 5-7 minutes. You may want to reduce heat to medium if too hot.

Add tadka to cooked dal and stir. Add lemon juice and sweetener (if using) and simmer on medium or medium-low heat for another 10 minutes. Garnish with coriander leaves and serve.

Makes **2-4 servings.**

slightly slightly
–(V) +(P) +(K)

Granny's Dal

On Sundays, my grandmother would serve this with rice or chapatis for our large family gatherings. Urad dal has a calm, grounding effect on Vata, which is perfect for my highly active family!

2 cups whole urad dal
6 cups water (for soaking)
6 cups water (for cooking)
1 tsp salt
1 2½-cm piece ginger, sliced
1 tsp good oil (page 27)
5 cups water
1 green chili, slit at end (optional)
- *To reduce Pitta: use ¼ or omit*

Tadka:
2 tsp good oil (page 27)
¾ cup onions, sliced
1 tsp ginger, minced
1-2 green chilies, minced
- *To reduce Pitta: omit*

1 tsp salt
- *To reduce Pitta: use less or omit*

¼ cup coriander leaves, chopped (for garnish) (optional)

In a large bowl, soak urad dal in water for at least 4 hours or overnight. Drain before cooking. In a large pot, combine soaked dal and remaining dal ingredients and bring to a boil. Reduce heat to medium-low and simmer until done, about 1 hour. Add a little water as needed if liquid starts to dry out.

In a medium frying pan on medium-low, heat oil. Add onions, ginger, green chilies, and salt, and sauté until onions are caramelized, about 8-10 minutes.

When dal is ready, remove ginger slices and whole chilies and place in a serving dish. Sprinkle tadka on top, garnish with coriander, and serve.

Makes **6-8 servings.**

slightly
ø(V) +(P) −(K)

Simple Brown Masoor Dal

Brown or green lentils cook fast and are very satisfying. The cumin and coriander calm all the *doshas*. I often prepare this dish when I return from a run, and by the time I am out of the shower it is ready. Caution: do not overcook these lentils as they will become too mushy. Serve with chapatis or rice, and yogurt.

1 cup brown or green lentils
3 cups water or vegetable stock (page 94)
⅓ cup onions, chopped
¾ cup tomatoes, chopped
1 tsp tomate purée (optional)
1 tsp ginger, minced
1 tsp good oil (page 27)
A pinch of asafoetida (optional)
¼ tsp turmeric
¾ tsp ground cumin
¾ tsp ground coriander
¼ tsp garam masala
¼ tsp green chilies, chopped, or cayenne pepper
- *To reduce Pitta: omit*

½ tsp salt, or to taste
1 tsp jaggery (or sweetener)
2 tbsp lemon juice
¼ cup coriander leaves, chopped (for garnish)

In a medium pot on high heat, bring lentils and water to a boil. Add all remaining ingredients except jaggery, lemon juice, and coriander leaves. Reduce heat and simmer for approximately 20 minutes, or until lentils are done, adding more water if necessary. Add gur and lemon juice, mixing well to dissolve gur. Adjust for seasoning. Sprinkle with coriander leaves and serve.

Makes **2-3 servings.**

Variation:

- Add 1 cup chopped vegetables to cook with other ingredients.

slightly
ø(V) –(P) –(K)
(D)

Quick & Easy Red Masoor Dal

These lentils are orange in their dried form and turn yellow once cooked. This is a great recipe if you're in a hurry or have unexpected guests. It has a light sweet and sour flavour and makes a balanced meal when served with rice or chapatis, yogurt, and a green salad.

1 cup red lentils (no need to be soaked)
3 cups water
1 tsp salt
A pinch of asafoetida (optional)
2½-cm ginger
1 green chili, slit at end
- *To reduce Pitta: use ¼ or omit*

½ cup tomatoes, diced
1 tsp tomato purée (optional)
½ cup onions, minced
¼ tsp turmeric
Juice of ½ a lemon
½ tsp jaggery (optional)
¼ cup coriander leaves (for garnish)

In a large pot, combine all ingredients except turmeric, lemon juice, jaggery, and coriander leaves. Bring to a boil, then reduce heat and simmer. Skim off froth with a slotted spoon. Add turmeric, stir, and cook until done, about 20 minutes. You may add more water if dal seems too dry. Add lemon juice and jaggery (if using), and stir to dissolve. Garnish with coriander leaves.

Makes **3-4 servings.**

slightly

+Ⓥ +Ⓟ −Ⓚ

Chana Dal

Chana dal is a robust and tasty lentil that is yellow in colour like tur dal, but can be heavier to digest, so only eat when your body has a strong digestive fire. Serve with chapatis or rice, a zucchini dish, and raitas for a complete meal.

2 cups chana dal

Tadka:

2 tbsp good oil (page 27)
1½ tsp whole cumin seeds
1½ cup tomatoes, chopped
1½ tsp ground coriander
¼ tsp turmeric
1 tsp garlic, minced
- *To reduce Pitta: omit*

1-2 tsp ginger, minced
Salt to taste
1-2 tsp green chilies minced, or cayenne pepper
- *To reduce Pitta: omit*

2 tbsp tomato paste
1 tsp sweetener (optional)
2 tbsp lemon juice, or to taste
½ cup coriander leaves, chopped (for garnish)

Soak and cook chana dal (page 31). In a medium frying pan on medium-high, heat oil. Add cumin seeds and let sizzle for 10 seconds. Add remaining ingredients except sweetener, lemon juice, and coriander leaves. Reduce heat to medium and sauté until tomatoes soften and spices are well cooked, about 8-10 minutes.

Add tadka to cooked dal and mix over medium heat. Cook for 5 minutes, then add lemon juice and sweetener (if using). Garnish with chopped coriander leaves.

Makes **6-8 servings.**

slightly
−(V) −(P) +(K)

Coconut Vegetable Tofu Medley

This is a complete meal when served with rice and includes all of the essential Ayurvedic tastes. I created this dish one day using whatever ingredients I had in the kitchen and it has since become a favourite. In Ayurveda, coconut is considered a sweet taste that calms Vata and cools down Pitta. It also is known to give strength, building Kapha properties.

1 tsp good oil (page 27)
- *To reduce Vata: add an extra tsp*

⅓ cup onions, chopped
1 clove garlic, minced
1 tsp ginger, minced
¼ tsp turmeric
1 tsp salt, or to taste
1 green chili, minced
- *To reduce Pitta: use ¼ tsp or omit*

1 cup red bell peppers, diced
1 cup yellow bell peppers, diced
3 cups zucchini, quartered and sliced
- *To reduce Kapha: use broccoli instead*

2 cups medium tofu, cubed
½ cup coconut milk
Juice of 1 lemon
1 tsp sweetener (optional)
¼ cup coriander leaves, chopped (for garnish)

In a medium pot on medium-high, heat oil. Add onions and sauté for 1-2 minutes. Reduce heat to medium, then add garlic, ginger, turmeric, salt, and chili, and sauté for another 1-2 minutes. Add peppers and zucchini, cover with lid, and cook until almost done, 4-6 minutes. Add tofu, coconut milk, lemon juice, and sweetener (if using). Reduce heat to medium-low and simmer for another 5 minutes. Garnish with coriander leaves and serve.

Makes **3-4 servings.**

–Ⓥ –Ⓟ +Ⓚ

Tofu with Bok Choy & Yam Home Fries

My friend, Let, often fuses her traditional Philippino cuisine with our 'modern' ingredients. She once cooked this simple, tasty dish for lunch which left me feeling satisfied and energized without feeling heavy.

1 tsp toasted sesame oil
1 cup tofu, cubed
½ tsp ground arrowroot
¼ cup water
1 tsp soy sauce
½ tsp oyster sauce
1 cup bok choy (or pak choi), chopped
1 tsp *ghee*, (or good oil, page 27)
1 cup yams, peeled and sliced ¾-cm thick
Water, enough to cover the yams in the skillet

In a frying pan on medium-high, heat oil. Add tofu and brown for about 2 minutes. In a cup or small bowl, dissolve arrowroot in water and stir. Add to tofu along with soy sauce and oyster sauce, mixing well. Bring to a boil, stirring constantly as it thickens, about 1 minute. Immediately add bok choy, cover with lid, reduce heat to medium, and cook for 3-5 minutes, or until done.

In another frying pan on high, heat *ghee* (or oil). Add yams and brown on each side. Add enough water to cover yams and cook, covered, for 4 minutes. Remove lid and continue to cook until most of the water evaporates. Serve immediately with the tofu and bok choy.

Makes **2 servings.**

Arrowroot is a starch made from the swollen roots of a plant native to the West Indies and South America. It is a wonderful, clear thickener used in gravies and sauces that is more easily digested than other thickening agents.

slightly

–(V) +(P) –(K)

Tandoori Tofu

After marinating in this delectable mixture overnight, the tofu becomes rich with flavour. *Tandoori Tofu* is great barbecued as well as baked, and can also be made into a tasty appetizer by cutting them into bite-sized squares and serving with toothpicks, *Taramind Chutney* (page 174), and yogurt.

1½ cups firm tofu, cubed
1 cup plain yogurt
- *To reduce Kapha: use a lighter version*

2 cloves garlic, minced
- *To reduce Pitta: use ½ clove or omit*

1 tsp ginger, minced
¼ cup coriander leaves, chopped
Juice of 1 lemon
½ tsp ground cumin
½ tsp ground coriander
¼ tsp turmeric
1 green chili, minced
- *To reduce Pitta: omit or use ¼ tsp*

¼-½ tsp garam masala
¾ tsp salt, or to taste
¼ cup coriander leaves, chopped (for garnish)

In a large bowl, combine tofu with remaining ingredients except coriander leaves and toss until well mixed. Cover and refrigerate overnight.

Set oven to broil. Place tofu pieces in a single layer on a baking sheet. Pour any remaining marinade over top. Place on upper rack in oven and broil, stirring until lightly browned on each side, 3-4 minutes. Garnish with coriander and serve.

Makes **4-6 servings (5 cubes per person).**

Rice

Almost every Indian meal includes rice. White basmati rice, known for its fragrance and delicious flavour, is the most common variety in Ayurvedic diets as it is easy and calming on the digestive system and benefits all *doshas*. (If reducing Kapha, eat in moderation.) When cooked al dente, basmati rice is also low on the Glycemic Index. Brown rice is high in fiber, B and E vitamins, and iron, and has some protein; however, it can aggravate Pitta and Kapha due to its heavier, moist qualities. If you feel you need to increase your fiber intake, use brown rice, but take note of how it affects your body and digestion.

Rice doesn't contain gluten, a protein in many grains that can be difficult for some to digest. This makes rice dishes suitable for those with gluten intolerance.

–Ⓥ –Ⓟ –Ⓚ
Ⓓ

Aromatic Basmati Rice

This is the rice most often eaten at Indian meals.

1 cup white basmati rice
2 cups water
2 cloves
- *To reduce Pitta: omit*

3 cardamom pods, slit at end
4 whole peppercorns
2 pieces cinnamon sticks 2½-5-cm long
Salt to taste

In a medium pot over high heat, combine all ingredients and bring to a boil. Reduce heat to simmer, cover with lid, and cook for 20 minutes.

Inform your guests that the whole spices are not to be eaten, as they are only there for flavouring. You may remove them before serving, but, if you leave them in they will continue to add flavour to the dish (and they look good too).

Makes **3-4 servings.**

Variation:

- *Cumin Rice:* Heat 1 tsp good oil, add cumin seeds and let sizzle for 10 seconds. Add all the ingredients of *Aromatic Basmati Rice* and cook as directed.

–Ⓥ –Ⓟ –Ⓚ Ⓓ

Saffron Rice

4 saffron strands (or ¼ tsp of whole cumin seeds)
2 tbsp water
1 cup basmati rice
2 cups water
Salt to taste

Saffron gives this rice dish a festive yellow colour. It adds a subtle flavour and is known to revitalize the blood and circulation, as well as alleviate migraine headaches. When buying saffron strands look for the brightest colour. They're the world's most expensive spice, but a little goes a long way!

In a bowl of water, soak saffron for 15 minutes. In a medium pot on high heat, combine saffron, (or cumin seeds) including water it was soaking in, and the remaining ingredients. Bring to a boil, then reduce heat to simmer, cover with lid, and cook for 20 minutes.

Makes **3-4 servings.**

Variations:

- Add 2 tbsp raisins (this will increase Kapha).
- Add 2 tbsp dried cranberries (this will increase Vata and Pitta).
- Add 2 tbsp slivered toasted almonds (this will increase Pitta and Kapha).

–Ⓥ –Ⓟ –Ⓚ
Ⓓ

Khichari

¼ cup split mung dal
½ cup basmati rice
2 cups water
Salt to taste
2 tsp flax or hemp oil
(or *ghee* or butter)

Khichari is used in Ayurveda for healing and cleansing the system. It is calming for all the *doshas*, especially Vata. The split mung dal and rice create a complete protein that strengthens and nourishes the body. Khichari is meant to be a bit softer and mushier than ordinary rice, I add about ½ cup water and cook it for about 5 minutes longer if I want it even softer and mushier. If using brown rice, cook for 45 minutes and let sit for another 10 minutes.

In a medium pot on high heat, combine all ingredients, except oil, and bring to a boil. Reduce heat to simmer, cover with lid, and cook for 25-30 minutes. Drizzle with oil before serving.

Makes **2-3 servings.**

Variations:

- Add ¼ tsp turmeric. Turmeric is a blood purifier and aids digestion of complete proteins. It reduces flatulence and inflammation, and is great for a sore throat. It also adds a lovely yellow colour.
- Add 1 piece cinnamon bark, 2 cloves, and 2 cardamom pods, slit at end, and cook with the other ingredients.

ØⓋ –Ⓟ –Ⓚ Ⓓ

Vegetable Rice Pullao

Pullao, has a rainbow of colours and is a wonderful way to get your vitamins and nutrients in one dish. The veggies in this pullao add a distinct flavour to the rice, because when they are cooked together their juices get absorbed in the grains.

1 cup hot water
1 tbsp oil
1 tsp whole cumin seeds
½ cup onions, chopped
1 tsp garlic, minced
- *To reduce Pitta: omit*

1 tsp ginger, minced
2 cups white basmati rice
1 green chili, slit at end
- *To reduce Pitta: omit*

1 cup potatoes, cubed
1 tomato, chopped
½ cup red bell peppers, cubed
1 cup green peas
- *To reduce Vata: use green beans*

¾ cup carrots, chopped
½ tsp turmeric
1 tsp salt, or to taste
¼ cup coriander leaves, chopped (for garnish)

In a medium pot on medium-high, heat oil. Add cumin seeds and let sizzle for 10 seconds. Add onions, garlic, and ginger, and sauté for 30 seconds. Add rice and stir until it is coated with oil. Add green chili, potatoes, tomato, peppers, peas, carrots, turmeric, and salt. Add water, enough to cover rice by 2½-cm. Bring to a boil, then reduce heat to simmer, cover with lid, and cook until done, about 20-25 minutes. Remove chili, mix well, and garnish with coriander leaves.

Makes **6-8 servings.**

Variation:
- Add ¾ cup tofu, cubed, at the same time as you add the vegetables.

slightly
−Ⓥ +Ⓟ −Ⓚ

Bean Pullao

This dish is full of flavour from the mixture of spices and yogurt that are fully absorbed by the rice during the cooking process.

1 tbsp grapeseed oil (or other good oil, page 27)
1 cup onions, thinly sliced
1½ cup tomatoes, chopped
1 cup plain yogurt
1 tsp garlic, minced
- *To reduce Pitta: omit*

1 tsp ginger, minced
2 tsp green chilies
- *To reduce Pitta: use only ½ tsp or omit*

½ cup coriander leaves, chopped
1 tsp ground coriander
1 tsp ground cumin
3 cloves
- *To reduce Pitta: omit*

4 peppercorns
3 cardamom pods, slit at end (optional)
2 cinnamon sticks 5-cm long
Salt to taste
2 cups azuki beans, cooked
2 cups basmati rice

In a medium pot on medium, heat oil. Add onions and cook until golden, 4-5 minutes. Add all other ingredients except beans and rice and sauté for 7-8 minutes, until tomatoes soften. Add beans and rice and mix well. Add enough water to cover rice by 2½-cm. Bring to a boil, then reduce heat to simmer, cover with lid, and cook for 20-25 minutes. Remove from heat and let sit for 5 minutes. Remove whole spices before serving.

Makes **6-8 servings.**

Vegetables

In Indian cooking, vegetable dishes, traditionally served in combinations of two or more, form an essential part of a meal. They can be prepared in many ways, providing a wide assortment of textures and spices that both stimulate the digestive juices and satisfy the *doshas*. This section includes mild vegetable dishes as well as some that are spicier to give your palate a tasty mix.

øⓥ øⓟ –ⓚ

Spinach & Broccoli Bhaji

1 tsp butter (or *ghee*)
2 tsp olive oil
1½ small onions, sliced
1 tbsp ginger, minced
1 green chili, slit at end (optional)
- *To reduce Pitta: omit*

5-6 cups spinach, chopped
1 head broccoli, roughly chopped
1 tsp salt, or to taste

The secret to this recipe is caramelizing the onions; the longer you take to cook them, the sweeter they get. Spinach cleanses the blood, clears the lungs, and is good for the eyes. It is packed with vitamins A and C, iron, and dietary fiber. Serve with chapatis or rice with onions, sliced radish, green chilies, and a yogurt raita.

In a large pot on medium-low, heat butter and oil. Add onions, ginger, and chili and sauté until onions caramelize, about 8 minutes. Add spinach, broccoli, and salt and cover with lid. Reduce heat to low and cook for 20-30 minutes. Remove from heat, then in a blender or food processor, purée (be careful when blending hot ingredients).

Makes **4 servings.**

slightly slightly
+(V) –(P) +(K)

Persian Greens

Garlic chives has a strong aromatic flavour that is fresh and zesty, resembling the subtle onion flavour of both chives and garlic. Pungent, warming, and stimulating, it is sometimes recommended to alleviate depression, and like garlic, it has antibiotic properties and promotes blood flow. Garlic chives are also a good source of calcium phosphates as well as other vitamins.

1¼ cups kidney beans
4 tbsp good oil (page 27)
1½ cups onions, minced
½ tsp turmeric
Freshly ground pepper to taste
1½ cups hot water
½ cup parsley, minced
1 cup spinach, minced
¼ cup garlic chives, minced
¼ cup fenugreek leaves, minced
1 tbsp mint leaves, minced
5 dried limes
3-4 tbsp lime juice, or to taste
Salt to taste

Soak kidney beans in water overnight or for at least 1 hour before cooking. In a pot on medium, heat 2 tbsp oil. Sauté onions until golden, about 6 minutes. Add turmeric and sauté for 1 minute. Add kidney beans, pepper, and hot water. Cover with lid and simmer gently until beans are half cooked.

In a separate pot on medium, heat 2 tbsp oil. Add parsley, spinach, garlic chives, and fenugreek leaves and cook until spinach is wilted, about 3-4 minutes. Add to beans and then add dried limes. Cover with lid, reduce heat to medium-low, and simmer for 30 minutes. Add lime juice and salt. Simmer for another 5-10 minutes. Serve with rice.

Makes **4 servings.**

slightly slightly

+Ⓥ +Ⓟ −Ⓚ

Curried Green Peas

Find out why no one has to say, 'Eat your peas!' at Indian dinner tables. Apart from enriching the flavour, spices warm the cool peas and make them calming for Vata. Serve with rice.

1 tbsp good oil (page 27)
½ cup onions, minced
1 tsp garlic, minced
- *To reduce Pitta: omit*

1 tsp ginger, minced
1 tsp ground cumin
1 tsp ground coriander
½ tsp turmeric
¼-1 tsp cayenne pepper
- *To reduce Pitta: omit*

2 cups tomatoes, diced
- *To reduce Pitta: omit*

1 tbsp tomato purée
- *To reduce Pitta: omit*

1¼ tsp salt, or to taste
3 tbsp coriander leaves, chopped
4 cups green peas
1 cup water
Juice of ½ a lemon
½ tsp garam masala

In a pot on high, heat oil. Add onions, garlic, and ginger. Reduce heat to medium and sauté until onions are golden, about 3-5 minutes. Add cumin, coriander, turmeric, and cayenne and sauté for another 30 seconds. Add tomatoes, tomato purée, salt, and 1½ tbsp chopped coriander leaves. Sauté for 5 minutes until tomatoes soften. Add peas and mix well. Add water, increase heat to high, and bring to a boil. Cover with lid, reduce heat, and simmer until done, about 10 minutes. Adjust for salt and add lemon juice. Sprinkle with garam masala and coriander leaves. To serve this with chapatis, this recipe should be less liquid, so add ¼ cup plus one tbsp water instead of 1 cup. If this is too dry, add a little more water, 1 tbsp at a time.

Makes **4 servings.**

Variation:

- *Mutter Paneer:* Follow the recipe above, then add ¾ cup paneer, cubed, just before adding garam masala and chopped coriander leaves.

slightly

+(V) −(P) −(K)

Pea & Mushroom Curry

The spices add flavour and aid digestion in this pea and mushroom medley.

1 tbsp good oil (page 27)
½ tsp black mustard seeds
¾ cup onions, minced
½ tsp turmeric
1 tsp garam masala
⅓ cup plain yogurt
1 tsp salt, or to taste
3 cups green peas
3 cups mushrooms, sliced

In a pot on medium-high, heat oil. Add mustard seeds, cover with lid, and let pop for 30 seconds. Add onions, reduce heat to medium-low, and sauté until golden, about 6-8 minutes. Add turmeric and garam masala, and stir for about 30 seconds. Add yogurt and salt, increase heat to medium-high, and bring to a boil. Reduce heat to medium and add peas. Cook for 3 minutes, then add mushrooms. Cover with lid and continue cooking for 10-15 minutes, until peas and mushrooms are done. Adjust for salt and serve.

Makes **4 servings.**

ø(V) ø(P) –(K)
(D)

Alu Methi

My family always quickly polishes off this dish. The fenugreek provides the bitter taste that is prized for cleansing the liver and creating clarity of mind and sight. They reduce flatulence, rheumatism, chronic coughs, dysentery, loss of appetite, diabetes and hypoglycemia. Fenugreek leaves a good source of protein and are rich in essential amino acids.

1 tbsp good oil (page 27)
½ tsp whole cumin seeds
1 cup onions, minced
1-2 green chilies, minced
- *To reduce Pitta: reduce or omit*

1 tsp ginger, minced
½ tsp turmeric
Salt to taste
1 cup tomatoes, diced
- *To reduce Pitta: omit*

4 cups potatoes, boiled, peeled, and diced
1 cup fenugreek leaves, chopped

In a pot on medium-high, heat oil. Add cumin seeds and let sizzle for 10 seconds. Add onions and sauté until just golden, about 3-4 minutes. Add chilies, ginger, turmeric, salt, and tomatoes and stir. Reduce heat to medium and cook until tomatoes soften, about 5-7 minutes. Add potatoes and fenugreek leaves and cook until fenugreek wilts, about 5 minutes. Stir to mix well, then serve.

Makes **4 servings.**

Variation:

- *Potato & Spinach Curry:* Add 4 cups spinach, chopped and ½ cup water in place of fenugreek leaves and cook for 2-3 minutes longer.

+(V) +(P) −(K)

Eggplant Bharta

In my opinion, this is the pièce de resistance in an Indian vegetarian menu. The secret is broiling the eggplant until it is very soft, sizzling the cumin seeds, and slow-cooking the onions and vegetables.

2 large eggplants
A little olive oil to rub on eggplants
2 tbsp olive oil
- *To reduce Kapha: use light*

1½ tsp whole cumin seeds
2 medium onions, chopped
1½ tsp ginger, minced
3 medium tomatoes, diced
1 tsp salt, or to taste
1-2 tsp green chilies, minced
- *To reduce Pitta: use ½ tsp or omit*

¼ cup coriander leaves, chopped (for garnish)

Set oven to broil. Wash and dry each eggplant. Pierce both ends with a fork, coat eggplant all over with oil, and broil for about 20 minutes on each side, until very soft on all sides. Remove from oven and let cool completely. Scoop out eggplant pulp and chop or mash it. Set aside in a bowl and discard peel.

In a large frying pan on medium-high, heat oil. Add cumin seeds and let sizzle for 10 seconds. Add onions, reduce heat to medium, and sauté until onions are golden, about 5-7 minutes. Add ginger, tomatoes, salt, and chilies and cook until tomatoes soften, about 4-5 minutes. Add mashed eggplant, reduce heat to medium-low, and cook for another 10 minutes, stirring occasionally. Eggplant tastes especially good if you cook it until it begins sticking to the bottom of the pan. Garnish with chopped coriander leaves.

Makes **2-4 servings.**

–Ⓥ +Ⓟ –Ⓚ

Soft & Spicy Eggplant Curry

The soft texture of the eggplant is delicious when combined with peas and spices. Serve this on rice.

1 tbsp good oil (page 27)
1½ tsp black mustard seeds
1½ cups onions, chopped
1 tsp salt, or to taste
½ tsp turmeric
¼ tsp cayenne pepper, or to taste
⅛ tsp asafoetida (optional)
1 cup tomatoes, chopped
6 cups eggplant, cubed
1½ cups green peas
¾ cup water
1 tbsp coriander leaves, chopped (for garnish)

In a large pot on medium-high, heat oil. Add mustard seeds, cover with lid, and let pop for 30 seconds. Add onions, salt, turmeric, cayenne, and asafoetida and sauté until onions are golden, about 4-5 minutes. Add tomatoes and eggplant, mix well, cover with lid, and cook for 10 minutes. Add peas and water and cook for another 5 minutes, or until peas are done. Check for seasoning. Garnish with coriander leaves.

Makes **4-6 servings.**

Variation:

- Add 1 cup potatoes, cubed and ½ cup water along with tomatoes and eggplant.

−Ⓥ −Ⓟ øⓀ
Ⓓ

Zucchini & Squash Medley

My cousin's primary *dosha* is Pitta, when she needs to calm Pitta, she cooks this colourful and nourishing dish.

1-2 tbsp olive oil
2 cups zucchini, diced
2 cups squash, diced
1 tsp ground coriander
Salt to taste
Juice of ½ a lime
¼ cup coriander leaves, chopped (for garnish)

In a frying pan on medium-high, heat oil. Add zucchini and squash and sauté for 4-5 minutes, tossing regularly. Reduce heat to medium, add coriander, stir, cover with lid, and cook for about 5-7 minutes, until vegetables are soft. Add salt and lime juice, toss, and garnish with chopped coriander leaves.

Makes **2-4 servings.**

+Ⓥ −Ⓟ −Ⓚ

Broccoli, Cauliflower & Potato Bhaji

An adaptation of the cauliflower *bhaji*. This is one of the tastiest ways to eat it.

2 tsp good oil (page 27)
¾-1 cup onions, quartered
1 tsp ginger, minced
¼ tsp turmeric
1 green chili, slit at end or minced
- *To reduce Pitta: use ¼ tsp or omit, or cayenne pepper to taste*

1 cup potatoes, thinly sliced
2 cups broccoli, chopped into florets
2 cups cauliflower, chopped into florets
Salt to taste
½ tsp garam masala
Freshly ground pepper to taste
¼ cup coriander leaves, chopped (for garnish)

In a large frying pan on medium, heat oil. Add onions, ginger, turmeric, and chili and sauté for 2-3 minutes, until onions start to soften. Add potatoes, broccoli, and cauliflower. Mix well, stir in salt, cover with lid, and cook until vegetables are softened, about 15 minutes. (If it needs more liquid, add up to ¼ cup water, but avoid if possible.) Stir in salt. Cook until done, about 15 minutes. Sprinkle with garam masala and pepper. Garnish with coriander and remove chili before serving.

Makes **4-5 servings.**

Slitting chilies releases their flavour and heat. Use a sharp knife, keeping the end intact. Chilies are always optional. If you have excess Pitta, use very little or omit.

slightly
ØⓋ +Ⓟ −Ⓚ

No Fuss French Green Beans

French green beans, a thin variety, are tender, sweet, and crisp when fresh (the only way to have them). This recipe preserves the natural flavour and freshness of the beans while adding colour and zest. The lemon and vinegar not only add extra zing, but provide the sour taste, which aids digestion.

5 cups French green beans
6 cups iced water
1 cup red bell peppers, finely diced
½ cup red onions, finely diced
- *To reduce Vata and Pitta: omit*

½ cup cheese, crumbled
4-5 tbsp olive oil
3 tbsp balsamic vinegar
Juice of ½ a lemon
¼ tsp dry mustard
Salt to taste
Freshly ground pepper to taste

In a large pot of boiling water, add beans. Reduce heat to medium-high and blanch for 3-5 minutes until tender and bright green. Remove beans and immediately plunge in a bowl of iced water to stop the cooking process. Drain beans and add to serving bowl. Add all remaining ingredients and toss well. Check for seasoning and serve.

Makes **6-8 servings.**

Variation:

- Sauté chopped onions in 1 tsp olive oil on medium heat for 4-5 minutes, then add to beans.

slightly
+(V) ø(P) −(K)

Karela

Bitter gourd is a diuretic, a great liver cleanser, and regulates blood sugar, alleviating diabetes. Bitter tastes are prized in Ayurveda for balancing salty, sour, and sweet flavours and helping people to see clearly. They calm Pitta and Kapha and stimulate Vata.

4 cups bitter gourd, peeled and sliced into ¾-cm rounds
2 tsp salt,
½ cup good oil
- *To reduce Kapha: use a light oil*

4 cups potatoes, peeled and sliced
1 cup onions, thinly sliced
2 cups tomatoes, diced
2 tsp tomato paste
1 tsp garlic, minced
- *To reduce Pitta: omit*

1 tsp ginger, minced
2 tsp green chilies, minced
- *To reduce Pitta: omit*

1 tsp ground cumin
1 tsp ground coriander
1 tsp garam masala
¼ tsp turmeric
A pinch of asafoetida
½ tsp cayenne pepper
- *To reduce Pitta: omit*

Salt to taste
2 tsp jaggery (optional)
Juice of ½ a lemon
½ tsp garam masala
¼ cup coriander leaves, chopped

In a large bowl, add gourd and sprinkle with salt. Place a plate with a heavy can on top and leave to sweat for 4 hours. Rinse well, then squeeze out excess liquid.

In a frying pan on medium-high, heat oil. Add gourd and fry on both sides for 3-4 minutes, until crispy. Remove from pan and set aside. Add potatoes to pan and fry on both sides until crispy. Remove from pan and set aside. Reduce heat to medium, add onions, and sauté until golden, about 5-7 minutes. Remove half the onions and set aside. Add remaining ingredients to pan except gur and lemon juice, and sauté for about 7 minutes. Return gourd, potatoes, and onions to pan and sauté for another 5 minutes. Add jaggery (if using), ensuring it dissolves. Add lemon juice and stir. Sprinkle garam masala and coriander and serve.

Makes **6-8 servings.**

-Ⓥ -Ⓟ -Ⓚ Ⓓ

Simply Delicious Asparagus

1 bunch thin asparagus (about 10-cm thick in diameter)
1 tbsp *ghee* (or butter)
¼ cup cheese, grated
Salt to taste
Freshly ground pepper to taste

Asparagus is a diuretic and is sweet, cooling, and astringent. It is full of vitamins A, B, and C, folate, and fiber. Always buy the thinnest, freshest stalks of asparagus. Here I include one of the simplest, tastiest dishes.

Set oven to broil. In a large pot of boiling water, add asparagus. Reduce heat to medium-high and cook for 4-5 minutes, until asparagus start to soften yet are still crisp. In a baking dish, place asparagus. Dot with *ghee* all over. Sprinkle with cheese, salt, and pepper. Broil for 2-3 minutes or until cheese starts to brown. Serve immediately.

Makes **4 servings.**

+(V) +(P) −(K)

Grandma's Turnip Curry

Turnips are packed with vitamin C. When buying, choose smaller ones if possible, as they are often sweeter and softer. After cooking this, my neighbour Janis, who is a passionate vegetarian cook, said, 'It was just perfect.' Serve with rice or chapatis.

2 tsp good oil (page 27)
½ tsp whole cumin seeds
1 small onion, chopped
1 tsp garlic, minced
1 tbsp ginger, minced
8 cups turnips, peeled and cubed
¼ cup water
½ tsp turmeric
1 tsp salt
Cayenne pepper to taste
1 tsp sugar syrup (optional)

In a large pot on medium-high, heat oil. Add cumin seeds and let sizzle for 10 seconds. Add onions and sauté for 4-5 minutes until golden. Add garlic and ginger and sauté for 1 minute. Add turnips, water, turmeric, salt, and cayenne. Toss to mix. Reduce heat to medium, cover with lid, and cook for 30-40 minutes, until turnips are softened. If it needs more liquid, add a bit more water. Add sugar syrup and mash. Adjust seasoning and serve.

Makes **2-4 servings.**

+(V) ø(P) −(K)

Sweet & Sour Sambaro

This is a deliciously sweet, sour, and spicy vegetable dish that adds rich flavour and texture to a meal.

3 cups cabbage, chopped
1 tbsp salt
1 tbsp good oil (page 27)
2 dried red chilies
½ tsp black mustard seeds
½ cup carrots, julienned
2 green chilies, slit at end
½ tsp turmeric
1 tbsp jaggery
Juice of 1 lemon
Salt to taste

In a colander over a bowl or in the sink, add cabbage and sprinkle with salt. Place a plate and a heavy can on top and leave to sweat for 1-2 hours. Rinse cabbage and squeeze out excess moisture. Set aside.

In a large pan on medium-high, heat oil. Add dried red chilies and sauté until blackened. Add mustard seeds, cover with lid, and let pop for 30 seconds. Immediately add cabbage, carrots, green chilies, and turmeric and sauté for 3-4 minutes. If green chilies are too hot, remove white pulp and seeds before using. Add jaggery (if hard, mince first) and lemon juice. Sauté for another 1-2 minutes while gur dissolves. Remove from heat and place in a serving bowl to stop the cooking process. Taste for salt, adding if needed. Remove chilies before serving.

Makes **4-6 servings.**

slightly slighty

−Ⓥ +Ⓟ +Ⓚ

Spiced 'Buttermilk' Curry

Here is a low-fat version of a traditional family favourite that is quick to make. You'll love the flavour of the 'buttermilk' and spices with the sweet and sour tastes coming from the sweetener and lemon juice. Serve with rice or khichari. For a full-fat version, use 2 cups buttermilk and ¾ cup water instead of the yogurt-water mixture.

1¼ cups plain yogurt
1½ cups water
2 tbsp gram flour
1 tsp good oil (page 27)
½ tsp mustard seeds
½ tsp cumin seeds
¼ tsp fenugreek seeds
1 green chili, slit at end
- *To reduce Pitta: omit or use ¼ chili*

3-5 curry leaves
2 cloves
- *To reduce Pitta: omit*

½ tsp garlic, minced or pressed
1 tsp ginger, minced
¼ tsp turmeric
½ tsp jaggery (or other sweetener)
1 tsp salt, or to taste
¼ tsp cayenne pepper, or to taste
Juice of ½ a lemon
¼ cup coriander leaves, chopped, (for garnish)

In a medium mixing bowl with a whisk, blend yogurt, water, and flour until mixture is smooth. In a pot on medium-high, heat oil. Add mustard seeds, cover with lid, and let pop for 30 seconds. Add cumin seeds, fenugreek seeds, green chili, curry leaves, cloves, garlic, and turmeric, and sauté for 30 seconds. Add yogurt mixture and bring to a boil while stirring or whisking continuously. Reduce heat and simmer until mixture thickens (to the consistency of whipping cream) for about 10 minutes, continuing to stir. Add jaggery and stir until it dissolves. Then add salt, cayenne (if using), and lemon juice. The curry leaves, chili, and cloves can be discarded or left in for flavour. Garnish with coriander.

Makes **2-3 servings.**

−(V) +(P) −(K)

Curried Eggs

4 eggs, hard-boiled and halved
1 tbsp good oil
½ cup onions, chopped
¼ tsp turmeric
2 cups tomatoes, chopped
½ tsp cayenne pepper, or to taste
Salt to taste
Juice of ½ a lemon
¼ tsp garam masala
¼ cup parsley or coriander leaves, chopped (for garnish)

Eggs are a good source of balanced protein as they contain all the amino acids needed for the human body to function. Rich in minerals, iodine, phosphorus, zinc vitamins A, B, D, E, selenium, calcium, and iron they calm Vata, increase Pitta, and are balancing for Kapha when eaten once or twice a week. The spices, parsley, and coriander make the eggs easier to digest for Vata and Kapha. Eggs are hot, oily, and heavy in quality and can be difficult to digest according to Ayurveda, so make sure you eat these when your agni is good.

In a pot on medium-low, heat oil. Add onions and turmeric and sauté until onions turn golden, about 8-10 minutes, stirring often. Increase heat to medium and add tomatoes, cayenne, and salt. Cover with lid and cook until tomatoes soften, about 8-10 minutes. Add lemon juice and stir. Gently add cooked, halved eggs, keeping yolks intact. Carefully spoon tomato curry sauce over eggs. Sprinkle with garam masala and garnish with parsley or chopped coriander leaves.

Makes **2-4 servings.**

Whole grains, an important staple in the diets of people worldwide, are a rich source of minerals, fiber, and B vitamins. They are also grounding, as they produce serotonin in the brain (which helps to regulate our moods, sleep, and appetite, among other things) and stabilize our bodies' metabolism. All *doshas* benefit from eating some grains each day, but to reduce Kapha, eat smaller portions.

Breads and Grains

Hot buttered chapatis are a warm, soothing component to any Indian meal; adding spices, stuffing them, and using a variety of fibrous flours offer a rich assortment of flavours and textures. People who omit white or wheat flour from their diets will especially benefit from this section, as most of the recipes use alternative flours.

−Ⓥ −Ⓟ +Ⓚ

Whole Wheat Chapatis

Making chapatis can be a therapeutic activity, with all the kneading and rolling. Serve with a variety of entrées or for breakfast with a little *ghee* and honey or jam. Whole wheat is a grounding, moist grain that can balance ingredients such as beans and lentils.

2 cups whole wheat flour
½ tsp salt (optional)
1½ tbsp *ghee*
- *To reduce Kapha: use light oil*

1 cup boiling water (may need another tbsp)

In a bowl, combine flour and salt, and *ghee*. Pour water and mix with a wooden spoon; let sit until mixture cools. Once cooled, knead to form a firm, smooth dough. Cover and let sit for 5 minutes. Knead again lightly for another 4-5 minutes. Divide into 10 evenly-sized balls and place on a plate.

On a lightly floured surface with a rolling pin, roll out each ball evenly into 14-cm circle. In a dry heavy-bottomed (*tawa*) on non-stick frying pan on medium heat cook each chapati. When it begins to bubble, after about 1 minute gently press edges with a spatula to allow it to gather air and rise. Flip and cook the other side for 1 minute. Repeat with remaining dough. The more the chapatis bubble and rise, the lighter they are.

Makes **10 chapatis.**

slightly
+Ⓥ –Ⓟ –Ⓚ

Spelt & Gram Flour Chapatis

The combination of fresh coriander with the gram flour makes it hard to stop eating these chapatis. These are delicious dipped into plain yogurt or eaten with curries.

½ cup gram flour
½ cup spelt flour
½ tsp salt
1 tbsp coriander leaves, chopped
¼ cup water
1 tbsp buttermilk
1 tsp good oil (page 27)

In a large bowl, combine flours, salt, coriander, water, buttermilk, and oil. Knead mixture until it forms a smooth dough. If too sticky, add more spelt flour, 1 tbsp at a time. Divide mixture into 6 evenly-sized balls. On a lightly floured surface with a rolling pin, roll out balls into 14-cm circles.

In a dry heavy-bottomed (*tawa*) on non-stick frying pan cook each chapati by placing it top-side down. When it begins to bubble, after about 1 minute, gently press edges of chapati with a non-metal spatula as this allows it to gather air or rise. Flip and cook the other side for 1 minute. Repeat with remaining dough. Stack chapatis on top of each other coated with a little ghee, to prevent sticking.

To vary this recipe, add ½ tsp fresh green chilies, minced. (To reduce Pitta: omit.)

Makes **6 chapatis**

+(V) +(P) −(K)

Corn Chapatis

This is a rustic Indian farmer's flat bread. They are wonderful eaten with vegetable bhajis and curries.

1½ cup ground corn flour
½ tsp salt
1 tbsp *ghee* (or olive oil)
  • *To reduce Kapha: use*
1 tbsp plain yogurt (optional)
½ cup cold water (may need more)

In a large bowl, combine corn flour, salt, *ghee*, and yogurt then mix. Add water, 1 tbsp at a time, and knead to form a dough. If too moist, add more corn flour, 1 tbsp at a time; if too dry, add more water, 1 tbsp at a time. Divide dough into 6 evenly-sized balls. Rub hands with a little oil and on a lightly floured surface, shape balls into 12-cm flat circles.

In a dry heavy-bottomed (*tawa*) or non-stick frying pan on medium-high heat, cook each chapati for 2-3 minutes on each side. Repeat with remaining dough. If pan gets too hot, reduce heat. Experiment to determine the optimal heat to cook them. Stack chapatis on top of each other in dish, separate with wax paper or coat with a little *ghee*, to prevent sticking.

Makes **6 Chapatis.**

To get rid of ama, (toxins) from your body, add these ingredients to your dough when you add the salt: 1/8 tsp asafoetida; 3/4 tsp whole cumin seeds; a pinch of black pepper; ½ tsp ginger, minced; 1½ tsp turmeric; 1½ tsp ground coriander; and 3 tsp honey.

+Ⓥ øⓅ −Ⓚ

Traditional Rotlo

Millet flour is dark gray in colour, high in iron and B vitamins. This is dry, which reduces Kapha, and is known to help offset cold symptoms.

1¼ cups millet flour
½ tsp salt
2 tsp grapeseed or olive oil (or *ghee*)
- *To reduce Kapha: use 1 tsp*

¼ cup cold water

In a large bowl, combine all ingredients and knead until you form dough with the consistency of wet clay. If too dry, add more water, 1 tbsp at a time; if too mushy, add more flour, 1 tbsp at a time.

On a lightly floured surface, with a rolling pin or the palms of hands, flatten dough into an 20-cm circle. If it gets crumbly or starts to fall apart, wet your fingers and press it back together.

Lift it off the surface with a large, flat spatula so that it does not break apart. In a dry heavy-bottomed (*tawa*) or non-stick frying pan on medium-high heat, cook rotlo for 2-3 minutes, then flip over and cook other side for 2-3 minutes until slightly brown. Note that the rotlo is quite solid and will not bubble up or rise when cooking. Flip again if necessary; if pan is too hot, reduce heat. It is ready when both sides are crisp and brown. Cut into quarters and serve.

Makes **2-4 servings.**

−Ⓥ +Ⓟ +Ⓚ

Mooli Roti

Serve each roti with 2-3 tbsp plain yogurt and 1 tsp of green chutney.

4 cups whole wheat flour
9 tbsp *ghee*
1 cup cold water

Filling:
3 cups radish, grated
1½ tsp salt
1½ tsp green chilies, minced, or to taste
- *To reduce Pitta: omit*

¼ cup coriander leaves, chopped
1½ tsp ginger, minced
1 tbsp lemon juice
¼ cup *ghee*, melted (for brushing)

For filling: In a large bowl, combine all ingredients and mix well.

For roti: In a large bowl, combine flour and *ghee*. Add water and knead until it forms a firm, smooth dough. If too dry, add more water, 1 tbsp at a time, and knead again. Set aside in a bowl, covered, for 30 minutes.

Divide dough into 12 evenly-sized balls. On a lightly floured surface with a rolling pin, roll out dough into 12½-cm circles. Place 1/12th of the filling into the center of each circle. Fold the edges over and pinch them together to enclose the filling, then pat into a flat circle. Gently roll them out again into 15¼-cm circles.

In a dry heavy-bottomed (*tawa*) or non-stick frying pan on medium-high heat, cook roti for about 1 minute. Flip over and cook other side. Brush with a little melted *ghee*, cook for 2 minutes, then flip over again. Brush other side with melted *ghee* and cook for 1 minute, until lightly brown on both sides.

Makes **12 rotis.**

slightly
+(V) +(P) −(K)

Upma

1 cup yellow millet
1 tbsp *ghee* (or olive oil)
1 tbsp black mustard seeds
5 curry leaves
¼ tsp turmeric
1 tsp green chilies, minced
- *To reduce Pitta: omit*

½ cup onions, chopped
½ tsp salt
3 cups water
- *To reduce Vata: add an extra ½ cup*

Sprig of parsley (for garnish)

Millet has been a part of Indian diets for thousands of years, and is a staple in the diet of the Hunza people, who live in the foothills of the Himalayas and known for their long life spans. Toasting millet before using removes allergens, glutamine, and other Kapha qualities of this grain.

Preheat oven to 180°C. In a non-stick baking pan, place millet and toast for 7-8 minutes, until slightly brown. Remove from oven and set aside. In a pot on medium-high heat, melt *ghee*. Add mustard seeds, cover with lid, and let pop for 30 seconds, then immediately add curry leaves, turmeric, chilies, and onions. Reduce heat to medium-low and sauté until onions are golden brown. Add salt and water, increase heat, and bring to a boil. Gently add toasted millet, stirring constantly to avoid lumps. Allow mixture to come to a boil for 1-2 minutes. Reduce heat to low, cover with lid, and cook for 25-30 minutes, or until millet is light and fluffy. If the millet is not yet done you can add an extra ¼ cup of water. Remove from heat and serve immediately.

Makes **4-6 servings.**

It's possible to enjoy a wide range of tempting desserts on an Ayurvedic diet, so long as you use healthy ingredients. This section also includes contemporary takes on traditional Indian desserts like *Sweet Shikand* (pages 162), and *Traditional Indian Rice Pudding with Nuts* (page 158).

Desserts

Sugar was once considered a rare and costly commodity. Today, it is easily refined and stored, so we consume more than we should; much of the excess sugar eaten today is hidden in processed and packaged foods. Be aware that sugar creates a nutritional debt in the body that must be compensated by increasing your intake of vitamins, minerals, protein, and healthy fats that are all necessary to burn off sugar.

−Ⓥ −Ⓟ +Ⓚ

Traditional Rice Pudding with Nuts

A perfect dessert when you have leftover rice. The spices warm the cooling milk.

1 cup rice, cooked and mashed
4 cups whole milk
- *To reduce Kapha: use low-fat or goat's milk*

¼ tsp nutmeg
¼ tsp ground cinnamon
4 tbsp sweetener
3 tbsp raisins
1 tsp pistachios, coarsely chopped (for garnish)
1 tsp almonds, coarsely chopped (for garnish)

In a large pot on high heat, combine all ingredients except nuts, and bring to a boil. Reduce heat and simmer, stirring occasionally, for 20 minutes. Garnish with nuts and serve.

Makes **4 servings.**

Variation:

- Apart from adding a lovely subtle flavour and rich colour, saffron is a digestive aid and reduces food allergies. Add ¼ tsp broken saffron strands to 2 tbsp milk and set aside for 10 minutes. Then add with other ingredients to the pot.

slightly slightly

–Ⓥ +Ⓟ +Ⓚ

Light Carrot Halva

Gently cooking the carrots reveals the depth of their sweetness. In this recipe, the spices warm the carrots while the reduced milk, cream, and nuts enrich the flavour.

¼ tsp saffron strands, broken
2 tbsp whole milk
- *To reduce Kapha: use low-fat or goat's milk*

1 tbsp good oil
1 tbsp *ghee* (or butter)
3 cloves
4 cardamom pods, slit at end
2-3 pieces cinnamon bark (5-cm long)
1 kg cups carrots, grated
1 cup whole milk
- *To reduce Kapha: use low-fat or goat's milk*

½ cup cream
½ cup sweetener
10 almonds or pistachios (or combination), coarsely ground (for garnish)

In a small bowl, soak saffron strands in 2 tbsp milk. In a medium pot on medium, heat oil and *ghee*. Add cloves, cardamom pods, and cinnamon bark and stir for 1 minute. Add carrots and cook for 25-30 minutes, stirring frequently so carrots are not charred; add a little more *ghee* or oil if this occurs. Add milk, cream, and saffron-milk and cook for 10 minutes, stirring occasionally until liquid is absorbed. Add sweetener, reduce heat to low, and continue to cook until the mixture no longer clings to the side of the pot. Pour onto a flat serving plate and garnish with nuts. You may discard cloves, cardamom pods, and cinnamon bark or leave in as they continue to add flavour.

Makes **6-8 servings.**

Variation:
- Add ¼ cup raisins or currants when you add the sugar.

−Ⓥ −Ⓟ +Ⓚ

China Grass Pudding with Nuts

This is a refreshing dessert made with agar agar, a gelatin base sometimes called China grass. Serve with fruit, or on its own.

- 2½ tbsp agar agar flakes
- 1 cup water
- 1 cup sweetener
- 4 cups whole milk
  - *To reduce Kapha: use low-fat or goat's milk*
- 1 cup whipping cream
- 1 tsp vanilla extract (or a few drops of rose water)
- 1 tbsp almonds, slivered
- 1 tbsp pistachios, coarsely ground (for garnish)

In a large pot on high heat, combine agar agar and water and bring to a boil for 2 minutes while stirring until agar agar dissolves. Add sweetener and stir to dissolve. Add milk and whipping cream and cook for 2 minutes, stirring constantly. Remove from heat. Add vanilla extract and let cool slightly. Pour into a serving bowl. When completely cooled, garnish with nuts and refrigerate until firm, about 4 hours.

Makes **6-8 servings.**

Variation:

- Add ¼ tsp broken saffron strands to milk and let sit for 10 minutes before adding to pot.

–Ⓥ –Ⓟ –Ⓚ
Ⓓ

Fruity 'Jello'

This is a light, simple dessert that is good for you!

2 cups fruit of your choice, sliced or chopped
1 cup water
1 tbsp agar agar flakes
1½ cups apple juice

Place fruit in a serving bowl. In a medium pot on high heat, combine water and agar agar and bring to a boil for 2-3 minutes while stirring until agar agar dissolves. Remove from heat, add apple juice, and stir. Pour over fruit. Refrigerate until it sets, about 45-60 minutes.

Makes **4 servings.**

Made from seaweed, agar agar is a powerful, natural, flavourless gelatin that looks like transparent straw. Medicinally, it alleviates constipation.

−(V) +(P) +(K)

Sweet Shrikand

Saffron adds a subtle flavour and a warm pale yellow hue to this sweetened sour cream dessert. When combined with a hint of cardamom and garnished with almonds, this shrikand is a finger-licking delight.

2 cups light sour cream
4 tbsp sugar
¼ tsp ground cardamom
¼ tsp saffron strands, broken
2 tbsp almonds, coarsely ground
1 tsp almonds, coarsely ground (for garnish)
3 mint leaves (for garnish)

In a bowl, combine all ingredients except for garnishes, and mix well. Refrigerate for at least 3 hours so saffron has time to colour and flavour the dish. Before serving, stir to mix again. Garnish with almonds and mint leaves and serve.

Makes **4 servings.**

Use all ingredients from the *Sweet Shrikand.* Substitute 1 cup cheese and 1 cup whipping cream for the sour cream and add an extra tbsp of ground almonds. Then add from variations below:

- Mix 2 tbsp grated coconut and/or ½ tsp fennel seeds into shrikand.
- In a pot on medium-high, heat ½ tsp *ghee*. Add ¼ tsp freshly ground black peppercorns and ¼ tsp cinnamon, then add 1 cup chopped pear and cook until pear softens (may need 2 tbsp water). Mix into shrikand. (A little *ghee* helps Kapha to digest fruit when mixed with dairy.)

slightly

–(V) –(P) +(K)

Saffron, Raisins & Almond Vermicelli

The warm, fragrant flavours of cardamom and cinnamon combined with raisins and the yellow saffron make this dessert both a visual and tasty treat.

¼ tsp saffron strands, crushed
½ cup water (for soaking)
2 tbsp good oil (page 27)
6 cardamom pods, slit at end
2 cinnamon sticks
2 cups roasted vermicelli, broken into pieces
1 cup water
½ cup skim milk
- *To reduce Vata: use whole milk*

⅓ cup sweetener
1½ tbsp raisins
1½ tbsp almonds, coarsely ground (for garnish)

Preheat oven to 180°C. In a small bowl, combine saffron and ½ cup water and set aside. In a pot on medium, heat oil, add cardamom pods and cinnamon sticks and sauté for 30 seconds. Add vermicelli and sauté until it is evenly browned. Add 1 cup water, milk, sweetener, raisins, and saffron-water, increase heat, and bring to a boil. Remove from heat, pour into an ovenproof dish, cover with lid, and bake for 10 minutes. Remove lid and bake for another 10 minutes until liquid has evaporated. Remove cardamom pods and cinnamon sticks. Garnish with almonds and serve.

Makes **4 servings.**

−Ⓥ −Ⓟ +Ⓚ

Lapsi

This is a rich, grainy dessert that goes well with any meal.

2 tbsp *ghee* (or good oil, page 27)
1 cinnamon stick
1 cup cracked wheat
1 cup whole milk
- *To reduce Kapha: use low-fat, goat's, or soy milk*

2 cups water
¼ tsp saffron strands, broken (optional)
2 tbsp coconut, shredded
3 cardamom pods, slit at end
½-¾ cup sweetener
2 tbsp raisins
1 tsp almonds, coarsely ground (for garnish)
1 tsp pistachios, coarsely ground (for garnish)

Preheat oven to 150°C. In a pot on medium heat, melt *ghee*. Add cinnamon stick and cook for 30 seconds. Add cracked wheat and cook for about 6 minutes, stirring constantly. Add milk, water, saffron, coconut, and cardamom pods, and cook for 10 minutes, stirring occasionally. Add sweetener and raisins. Mix well and simmer until the liquid has been absorbed, continuing to stir, about 15 minutes. Remove from heat, pour into an ovenproof dish, cover with lid, and bake for 20 minutes. Garnish with almonds and pistachios and serve. You can remove cinnamon stick and cardamom pods before serving, or leave in as they continue to add flavour.

Makes **4-6 servings.**

−Ⓥ −Ⓟ +Ⓚ

Halwa

Halwa or kara or shira, is traditionally an offering, or 'prasad,' to the Gods. Eating as little as 1-2 tbsp of Kara can be very satisfying.

1 cup water
½ cup brown sugar or
¾ cup jaggery
¼ cup *ghee* (or butter)
1 cup whole wheat flour
1 cup whole milk
- *To reduce Kapha: use low-fat, goat's, or soy milk*

In a pot on high heat, combine water and sugar and bring to a boil, then reduce heat to medium. In another pot on medium heat, melt *ghee*. Add flour and stir constantly until mixture is golden brown. In a third pot on medium-high, heat milk until it just starts to boil, then remove from heat. Add water and sugar mixture to flour and *ghee* mixture. Whisk until smooth and thick. Add hot milk, reduce heat to low, and cook for about 20 minutes, stirring often.

Makes **4-6 servings.**

Variations:

- Add ¼ tsp broken saffron strands, ¼ tsp nutmeg, and ½ tsp ground cardamom to milk as it's heating.
- Garnish with 1 tbsp slivered almonds, 1 tbsp crushed pistachios, and 1 tsp white poppy seeds.

−Ⓥ −Ⓟ +Ⓚ

White Chocolate Cardamom Mousse

This cardamom-infused coconut milk combined with the chocolate makes this dessert irresistible. Chocolate contains anandamine, a protein used by our brain to produce pleasurable sensations. Ananda is the Sanskrit word for bliss.

6 cardamom pods, crushed
1¾ cup coconut milk
200 g white chocolate at room temperature, chopped into small pieces
1 pkt gelatin (for 4 servings)
1 tbsp icing sugar (optional)
2 tsp vanilla extract
2 egg whites

In a large pot on high, combine cardamom and coconut milk and bring to boil. Remove from heat, and remove pods with a slotted spoon (some cardamom bits may remain in pot). In a separate pot on very low heat, melt chocolate while stirring constantly. Return coconut milk to heat and sprinkle with gelatin while stirring to completely dissolve. Sift in sugar (if using), and stir to dissolve.

Remove coconut milk from heat, then add vanilla and melted chocolate. Whisk vigorously until well combined. Pour into a bowl, cover, and refrigerate for 30 minutes. In a medium bowl, beat egg whites until stiff. Remove mousse from refrigerator and fold in egg whites. Refrigerate for another 90 minutes to set.

Makes **4 servings.**

slightly
–Ⓥ +Ⓟ +Ⓚ

Creamy Extra Dark Chocolate Fondue

1 cup 70% cocoa mass dark chocolate, chopped or broken
1 cup soy milk (or whipping cream)
5-6 cups mixed fruit (e.g., orange segments, strawberries, sliced bananas, cherries, sliced pineapple)

Dark chocolate is a rich source of magnesium and has the bitter taste valued in Ayurveda. Chocolate is also acidic, but this is counterbalanced by the alkaline nature of the fruit. Studies indicate that dark chocolate with a h igh cocoa mass content (70% and above) is a good source of antioxidants. It is low on the Glycemic Index. A mood enhancer it stimulates the release of serotonin in the brain. It is often used in courtship rituals and called the food of love.

Place chocolate in an ovenproof bowl. In a medium pot on high heat, bring soy milk to a boil. Immediately remove from heat and pour over chocolate. Stir until smooth.

Arrange fruit on a platter. Serve with forks or fondue sticks to dip fruit into the chocolate.

Makes **6 servings.**

slightly
−Ⓥ +Ⓟ +Ⓚ

Carob Almond Cookies

Carob is a delicious, potassium-rich placebo for chocoholics.

½ cup coconut oil (or butter) (at room temperature)
½ cup sugar syrup
½ cup carob powder
1 cup finely ground almonds
- *To reduce Pitta: use blanched almonds, ground*

⅔ cup oat flour
Pinch of salt
⅓ cup carob chips (or nuts of your choice)

Preheat oven to 160°C. In a bowl, combine coconut oil and sugar syrup until well mixed. In a separate bowl, combine carob powder, almonds, oat flour, and salt, until evenly blended. Stir in carob chips. Add oil and sugar syrup mixture and stir until it forms a dark-coloured dough.

On a lightly greased baking sheet, place tbsp-sized balls of dough. Press down dough into circles and bake for 12 minutes or until edges are crisp. Allow to cool on a baking sheet before transferring to a cooling rack. These will be a bit soft on the inside, like brownies. Serve warm or cool.

Makes **14-18 cookies.**

−Ⓥ −Ⓟ +Ⓚ

Creamy Banana-Berry Ice

This recipe is delicious garnished with fresh berries, toasted coconut, or chocolate shavings.

4 bananas
Zest and juice of 1 lime
2 cups raspberries, blueberries, or strawberries
1 cup coconut cream

In a blender or food processor, combine bananas with the lime zest and juice and blend until soft and creamy, about 2 minutes. Add berries and coconut cream and continue to blend until desired consistency is reached. Serve immediately.

Makes **8-10 servings.**

Chutneys, pickles and raitas are an integral part of any Indian meal; they add colour and flavour to dishes and take them from merely good to sensational. They are also a good way to incorporate raw ingredients in your diet, as well as some of the six essential tastes (page 21) important to a balanced Ayurvedic meal. All the recipes here are relatively simple to prepare; in some, the vegetables, fruits, and spices are cooked lightly or marinated.

Chutneys, Pickles and Raitas

These are best served separately (ideally in small bowls decoratively placed on the table) and eaten in small quantities: one or two teaspoons of the chutneys and pickles, are enough for one person. Chutneys, pickles and raitas are useful for getting the digestive juices flowing, or as it is said in Ayurvedic terms, activating *agni*.

–Ⓥ +Ⓟ –Ⓚ

Tomato Chutney

¾ cup tomatoes, grated
3 tbsp tomato paste
½ tsp garlic, crushed
½ tsp ginger, crushed
1 tsp ground cumin
¾ tsp salt, or to taste
2 tsp lemon juice
½ tsp sugar
½ tsp chili powder, or to taste
1 tbsp olive oil

This chutney is a great replacement for ketchup with most dishes. Tomatoes are a rich source of vitamins A and C. If you want to make a full cup, double the quantity and use a larger frying pan, as the chutney should spread out in a thin layer on the pan as it cooks. This is a hot, pungent, and spicy chutney and only a little (about ½ tsp) adds great flavour to snacks and other dishes.

In a small frying pan on medium heat, sauté tomatoes. When liquid from tomatoes has almost evaporated, add tomato paste, garlic, ginger, cumin, salt, lemon juice, sugar, and chili powder. Sauté for 1 minute, then add oil, and stir for 30 seconds. Remove from heat and serve. If desired, store in a sealed container in the refrigerator for up to 2 weeks. The oil in this chutney works as a preservative. If for any reason you omit the oil, it will only last for up to 2 days.

Makes ½ **cup.**

–Ⓥ –Ⓟ –Ⓚ
Ⓓ

Coriander Mint Chutney

This chutney is balancing to all the *doshas*. Many Indian homes are never without it, as it adds flavour to numerous dishes and snacks.

- 6 cups coriander leaves
- 3 cups mint leaves
- 2 tsp salt, or to taste
- 3 tbsp olive or grapeseed oil
  - *To reduce Kapha: use a light version*
- 6 tbsp lime juice
- 1 tbsp sweetener (optional)
- 1-2 tsp olive oil (for preserving) (optional)

In a blender or a food processor, combine all ingredients and blend to a pulp. If chutney is too chunky, while blending add an additional 1-2 tbsp olive oil (will reduce Vata) or lime juice.

To preserve chutney, place in a sealed container and add 1-2 tsp of olive oil on top.

Makes **1½ cups.**

Variations:

- *Coriander Garlic Chutney:* Substitute mint leaves with 4-5 cloves garlic and add 1-3 green chilies.
- *Coriander Garlic Coconut Chutney:* Add 2-3 tbsp grated coconut to the above mixture. The chutney should have a paste-like consistency; if it needs more liquid, add 1-3 tbsp lime juice.

−(V) +(P) +(K)

Tamarind Chutney

½ cup tamarind pulp
2 cups water
½ cup jaggery
2-2½ tsp chili powder, or to taste
¼ tsp ground cumin

Tamarind pods has a distinctly rich, sour flavour; it is mouthwateringly delicious and enhances digestion. Gur is the first derivative of sugar cane with just the fiber and water removed, thus preserving its rich mineral and nutrient content — iron, magnesium, and potassium. *Tamarind chutney* is a great addition to any meal. It can also be used in place of lemon and honey for a sweet and sour flavour in dals or curries.

Rinse tamarind pulp once under running water and then, in a bowl, soak pulp in water for 30 minutes. In a medium pot on high heat, bring tamarind pulp and water to a boil. Reduce heat to simmer and add all other ingredients. Simmer for 5 minutes and remove from heat. Once cooled, rub with the back of a spoon through a sieve into a bowl. Make sure you rub as much tamarind juice as you can out of the pulp. Discard pits and threads. Store in a sealed container.

Makes **1½ cups.**

slightly
−(V) +(P) +(K)

Coconut Mint Chutney

A mere teaspoonful is delicious served with *Baked Pakoras* (page 56), snacks, and curries.

2 tbsp dry coconut, grated
½ cup plain yogurt
- *To reduce Kapha: may omit*

1-3 green chilies
- *To reduce Pitta: use ½ green chili or omit*

1 cup mint leaves
½ tsp salt
Juice of 1 lemon
½ tsp sweetener
¼ cup tomatoes, chopped (optional)
- *To reduce Pitta: omit*

In a blender or food processor, combine all ingredients and purée until smooth. Let mixture sit for at least 30 minutes before using to allow the coconut to absorb the liquid and start to thicken.

Makes **about 1 cup.**

−Ⓥ −Ⓟ −Ⓚ Ⓓ

Ripe Mango Chutney

3 ripe mangoes, diced
⅓ cup apple cider vinegar
¼ cup sugar syrup
Salt to taste
¼ tsp red chilies, minced

In many cultures, mangoes are considered the king of fruits; they are rich in vitamins A and C. Ripe mangoes are balancing to all three *doshas* when eaten in moderation. They are slightly warming, so Pittas should only eat in small amounts. I love the orange colour and rich flavour this fresh *chutney* adds to a meal.

In a pot on high heat, combine all ingredients and bring to a boil, then reduce heat and simmer for 15 minutes. Remove from heat and let cool. Store in a sealed container in the refrigerator for up to 1 week.

Makes **2 cups.**

slightly
−(V) +(P) +(K)

Lime Pickles

12 lemons, thinly sliced in circles
2-3 tsp salt
1 tsp turmeric
2 cups apple cider vinegar
3 cups sugar (jaggery or brown sugar)
4 bay leaves
4 cinnamon sticks
6 cloves
6 peppercorns
1 tsp whole cumin seeds
1 tsp cayenne pepper

Here is a delicious sweet and sour pickle that can be served with any curry dish. They are also often eaten in very small amounts at breakfast or with cheese and toast.

Spread out lime slices on a baking sheet, and sprinkle evenly with ½ the salt and ½ the turmeric. Turn each slice over and sprinkle evenly with rest of salt and turmeric. Let sit on the counter (or in the sun, if possible) for 2-3 days. In a pot on low heat, bring remaining ingredients to a simmer for 30 minutes until syrup thickens. Add lime slices, simmer for another 10 minutes, and remove from heat. Cool and store in a jar with a lid. Let this sit on the counter for 2 weeks before using and shake from time to time.

Make sure the syrup covers the lime slices by ¼-½-inch. If this reduces during the 2 weeks of storage, top up with vinegar.

Makes **2½-3 cups.**

slightly
−Ⓥ +Ⓟ −Ⓚ

Carrot Pickles

This is a 'must have' and a great way to add the raw ingredients essential to a balanced Ayurvedic meal.

3 carrots, sliced into 6-cm long thin sticks
½ tsp lemon juice
2 tbsp apple cider vinegar
1 tsp salt
½ tsp chili powder, or to taste
1 tsp yellow mustard seeds, crushed
2 slices ginger (optional)
2 green chilies, slit at end (optional)
¼ tsp turmeric (optional)

Combine all ingredients in a jar with a lid and shake well. Refrigerate for at least 2 hours before serving. Shake the jar from time to time.

If you do not have both lemon juice or vinegar on hand, you can use 2½ tbsp of either ingredient

Makes **2-2½ cups.**

–Ⓥ +Ⓟ +Ⓚ

Green Mangoes with Cayenne

2 raw green mangoes, diced
1 tsp salt, or to taste
½ tsp cayenne pepper, or to taste

Green mangoes add the sour taste that in small amounts aids digestion. To cut a mango, slice on either side of the seed or 'the bone' to create two slices. Then cut the remaining mango from around the seed. Discard the seed and dice each slice and the remaining flesh.

In a bowl, combine all ingredients and serve.

Makes **1½-2 cups.**

Raitas

Raitas are yogurt-based condiments that aid digestion. They are eaten in small quantities as an accompaniment to a meal. The spices increase the digestibility of the yogurt and the vegetables add texture, flavour, colour, and nutrients. Homemade yogurt does not increase Pitta as store-bought yogurt does. A little yogurt is beneficial for all constitutions.

–Ⓥ øⓅ +Ⓚ
Ⓓ

Homemade Yogurt

4 cups whole milk
2 heaping tbsp yogurt (at room temperature)

Freshly-made yogurt is full of beneficial bacteria that aids the digestion and kills some harmful bacteria. It also contains protein, B vitamin complex, calcium, potassium, phosphorus, and folic acid. People who have difficulty digesting milk often find fresh yogurt much easier to digest. People who have to take antibiotics often eat yogurt to replace the healthy bacteria that the antibiotics destroy.

In a pot on medium heat bring to a boil milk. Turn off heat and allow it to cool. Test with your finger; when it feels lukewarm, then pour milk into a very clean or sterilized bowl. Whisk in the yogurt. Cover bowl and let sit in a warm place where there is no draft (such as in the oven) for 8-12 hours before using. If you make this in the early evening, it will be ready for your breakfast when you wake up the next morning.

Save some of this yogurt to use for making the next batch.

Makes **4 cups.**

Here is remedy for an upset stomach: ¼ cup fresh yogurt and ¼ tsp whole cumin seeds, crushed.

−(V) +(P) +(K)

Cumin Raita

Cumin adds flavour to this raita and aids digestion. The cayenne gives it wonderful colour and a little punch. This is a simple, elegant way to complete your meal.

1 cup plain yogurt
¼ tsp whole cumin seeds, crushed
¼ tsp salt (optional)
Pinch of cayenne pepper (for garnish)
1 sprig mint or coriander leaves (for garnish)

In a bowl, combine yogurt, cumin, and salt. Sprinkle with cayenne and garnish with coriander.

Makes **1 cups.**

Variations:

- *Cucumber Raita:* Add grated ½ cucumber to the *Cumin Raita*!
- *Tomato Raisins Raita:* Add ¼ cup raisins and ½ cup diced tomatoes to the *Cumin Raita*.
- *Spinach Raita:* Add 3 cups chopped spinach to *Cumin Raita*.

–(V) +(P) +(K)

Coconut & Banana Raita

The mustard seeds mixed with the bananas and coconut add texture and flavour to this raita.

1¼ cups plain yogurt
1 cup bananas, sliced
1 tsp salt
1 tbsp olive oil
1 tsp black mustard seeds
2½ tbsp coconut, grated
1½ tbsp plain yogurt
1 tsp coriander leaves, chopped (for garnish)

In a bowl, combine 1¼ cups yogurt, bananas, and salt. Mix well and set aside. In a small frying pan on medium-high, heat oil. Add mustard seeds, cover with lid, and let pop for 30 seconds. Immediately add coconut. Stir for a few seconds, then add 1½ tbsp yogurt and continue stirring for a few more seconds until well mixed. Add mixture to a bowl of yogurt and bananas. Mix well. Garnish with coriander leaves, cover, and refrigerate for 1 hour before serving.

Makes **about 3 cups.**

According to Ayurveda, cold beverages suppress digestive juices and therefore are generally not recommended; instead, sip on room temperature water or warm tea with or without lemon. Also try to consume most of your liquids between meals for optimum hydration and cleansing. The milk beverages, *lassis*, and non-alcoholic cocktails in this section can be enjoyed at room temperature or slightly cooler.

Beverages

Beverages and teas can be snacks in themselves, select ones to calm your *dosha*, which changes with the season or time of day. Try some of these tasty, nourishing drinks instead of caffeinated tea or coffee and notice how your sense of well-being improves.

−Ⓥ −Ⓟ +Ⓚ

Almond Milk

If you need to reduce Kapha, drink a smaller amount and omit the sugar syrup, or use a little honey instead.

1 cup almonds
2 cups water (for soaking)
3 cups water (for blending)
Sugar syrup to taste (or honey) (optional)

In a bowl, soak almonds with 2 cups water overnight. The next morning, drain almonds and remove skins by pouring boiling water over them. Allow them to cool slightly, then pop off skin by squeezing each almond gently between your fingers. In a blender or food processor, blend almonds until very smooth. Add 3 cups water and continue blending for 3 minutes. Pour almond mixture through cheesecloth into a pitcher to drain off liquid; squeeze to extract any remaining liquid. Add sugar syrup to liquid and mix. Save leftover almond mixture to add to other recipes calling for nuts and seeds, or sprinkle over your breakfast cereal.

Makes **3 cups.**

Variations:

- *Spicy Almond Milk:* Add 2 tbsp ginger paste, 4 tsp poppy seeds and 1 tsp ground anise to 'Almond Milk'.
- *Almond Milk with Pistachios & Rose Water:* 4 cups Almond Milk, 2 tbsp unsalted, crushed pistachios, ¼ tsp ground cardamom, ⅛ tsp nutmeg, sweetener to taste, a few drops of rose water and a few strands of saffron (optional). In a pitcher, combine all ingredients, mix well, and serve.

slightly
−Ⓥ +Ⓟ −Ⓚ

How to Start Your Day Lemon Drink

I drink this fat-breaking and cleansing lemon tea first thing every morning.

Juice of ½ lemon
1 cup boiling water
Pinch of cayenne pepper (optional)
Sugar syrup to taste (or honey) (optional)

In a mug, combine all ingredients and stir.

Makes **1 servings.**

slightly slightly

−Ⓥ +Ⓟ +Ⓚ

Nice & Nutty Brown Rice Milk

This non-dairy milk is full of fiber and nutrients.

½ cup short-grain organic brown rice, uncooked
8 cups water
½ tsp salt

In a large pot on high heat, combine rice, water, and salt and bring to a boil. Reduce heat to a simmer, cover with lid, and cook for 1½ hours. Remove from heat, then in a blender or food processor, purée until smooth and serve. This will keep in the refrigerator for 7 days.

Makes **about 6 cups.**

Variations:

- Add melted, 70% cocoa mass dark chocolate.
- Add ground cinnamon to taste and sweeten with sugar.
- Add 1-2 tbsp of flax seeds to increase omega-3 oils and the nutritional value.

–Ⓥ øⓅ +Ⓚ

Pineapple & Coconut Cocktail

Feast your eyes and taste buds on this tropical treat.

3 cups pineapple juice
1 cup coconut milk
2 tsp sugar syrup (optional)
½ tsp lime juice
4 strawberries (for garnish)
4 mint leaves (for garnish)

In a pitcher, combine all ingredients except garnishes and mix well. Pour evenly into 4 glasses. Slit ends of strawberries to place on the lip of each glass and add a mint leaf on top of each cocktail, then serve.

Makes **4 servings.**

Variation:

- *Ginger Mint Cocktail:* 4 tsp roughly chopped ginger, ¼ cup roughly chopped mint leaves, ¼ cup lime juice, 4 tsp sugar syrup (or honey) and 4 cups water. In a blender or food processor, purée ginger into a paste. Add mint leaves and purée into a paste. Add all remaining ingredients and blend. Strain through cheesecloth and pour into glasses.

-Ⓥ -Ⓟ -Ⓚ
Ⓓ

Masala Chai Mix

Masala is a blend of flavourful spices added to chai, which is derived from the Chinese character for tea, cha (tea originated in China). Add this mix to a pot of tea (1/8-1/4 tsp per cup). Over time you may increase or decrease the various spices, depending on your taste.

1 tsp cloves
1 tsp freshly ground black pepper
1 tsp cardamom seeds
½ tsp nutmeg, grated
1 5-cm piece cinnamon bark (or 1 tsp ground cinnamon)
1 tsp ground ginger

In a dry frying pan on medium heat, combine all ingredients and toast for 3-4 minutes, stirring constantly. Remove from heat. In a coffee grinder (one that you don't normally use for coffee), grind masala in batches, then mix together and store in an airtight container.

Makes **about ¼ cup.**

–Ⓥ –Ⓟ –Ⓚ

Milky Masala Chai

Here is a recipe for the milky version of masala chai, now popular worldwide. Milk products in general increase Kapha and are good for balancing Vata. They are consumed with ginger, pepper, and other pungent spices to make them easier to digest for the other *doshas*.

3 cups water
1 cup milk (or soy milk)
½-¾ tsp Masala Chai Mix
1-2 tsp loose leaf black tea (or 1-2 tea bags)
Sweetener to taste

In a large pot on high heat, combine all ingredients. Bring to a boil, stirring to ensure milk does not burn, then reduce heat immediately and simmer for 5 minutes. Strain, add sweetener if desired, and serve.

Makes **4 servings.**

-Ⓥ -Ⓟ -Ⓚ
Ⓓ

Tea Fit for a Yogi

My mother discovered the recipe for this calming yet energizing tea.

- 6 small pieces cinnamon bark
- 1 tsp whole fenugreek seeds
- 1 tsp cardamom pods
- 1 tsp cloves
- 1 tsp whole peppercorns
- 2 tsp fennel seeds
- 2 tsp ginger, chopped

In a brown paper bag, crush all ingredients except for ginger by using a rolling pin.

In a large bowl, combine all ingredients and mix together. Use 1-2 tsp per pot of hot water and steep to your taste. Store leftover tea mixture in an airtight container.

Makes **4-5 tablespoons.**

–Ⓥ –Ⓟ –Ⓚ
Ⓓ

Lemongrass, Mint & Ginger Tea

A refreshing tea that's great any time, but especially during summer. I make this tea for dinners and retreats, letting it simmer in a big pot on the stove before guests arrive. They are always thrilled to be greeted by its soothing scent.

1 bunch mint leaves, chopped
2 sticks lemongrass
4 ginger tea bags (or 3 tbsp fresh ginger, chopped)
5 cloves
5 cardamom pods, slit at end
4-5 pieces broken cinnamon bark
8-10 cups water

In a large pot on high heat, combine all ingredients. Bring to a boil, then reduce heat and simmer for 5-10 minutes, depending on desired strength. Strain before serving.

Makes **8-10 servings.**

−(V) +(P) −(K)

Radish Tea

Flush fats out of your body with this tea.

¼ radish, roughly chopped
4 cups hot water

In a large pot on high heat, combine all ingredients. Bring to a boil, then reduce heat and simmer for 15-20 minutes. Remove from heat, strain, and serve.

Makes **3-4 cups.**

Variations:

- *Dandelion Tea:* Add 2 cups dandelions (flower, leaves and stems) instead of radish.
- *Parsley Tea:* Add 1 bunch fresh parsley and juice of 1 lemon instead of radish.
- *Turmeric Tea:* Combine 1 tsp turmeric, 4 cups boiling water and 2 tsp honey.

−Ⓥ −Ⓟ −Ⓚ
Ⓓ

Calming Ginger Tea

This tea is warming, good for calming the nerves, and delicious.

4 tsp ginger, chopped
4-6 cups water
Sugar syrup to taste (or honey) (optional)

In a large pot on high heat, combine ginger and water. Bring to a boil, then reduce heat and simmer for at least 5 minutes. Add sugar syrup and serve.

Makes **4 servings.**

Variation:

- *Garlic Ginger Tea:* 4 cloves garlic, pinch of cayenne pepper, 4 tsp fresh ginger, chopped, 4-6 cups water, sugar syrup to taste (or honey) (optional) and squeeze of lemon (to taste). In a large pot on high heat, combine garlic, cayenne, ginger, and water. Bring to a boil, then reduce heat and simmer for 30 minutes. Strain, serve with sugar syrup (if using) and a squeeze of lemon.

slightly
−(V) +(P) −(K)

Autumn Tea

This is a warming tea that's good for the throat and when you have a cold.

- 2 brown rice tea bags
- 2-3 cardamom pods, slit at end
- 2-3 cloves
- 2 cinnamon sticks
- ½ tsp turmeric
- 8-10 cups water

In a large pot on high heat, combine all ingredients. Bring to a boil, then reduce heat and simmer for 5-10 minutes, depending on desired strength. Strain before serving.

Makes **8-10 servings.**

–Ⓥ –Ⓟ –Ⓚ
Ⓓ

Cooling Summer Tea

I make this for my summer yoga retreats; everyone loves its soothing and refreshing flavour.

3 tbsp ginger, chopped
2 cinnamon sticks
3 cardamom pods, slit at end
½ bunch mint leaves
6 cups water
Honey to taste (optional)

In a large pot on high heat, combine all ingredients. Bring to a boil, then reduce heat and simmer for 5-10 minutes. Strain then serve in mugs. You may add more water to pot as ingredients get more potent and use same ingredients for a second round.

Makes **6 servings.**

−Ⓥ −Ⓟ −Ⓚ Ⓓ

Non-Alcoholic Mulled Wine

My father made this one day while entertaining at our family home. The sun had just gone down and a nice cool breeze was blowing. This drink was a perfect way to greet our guests.

- 4 cups unsweetened grape juice
- 2 cups unsweetened apple juice
- 2 cups unsweetened pineapple juice
- 1 cup unsweetened cranberry juice
- 4 tbsp sugar syrup (or honey) (optional)
- 1 10-cm cinnamon stick
- ¼ tbsp cloves

In a large pot on medium-low heat, combine all ingredients and slowly bring to a boil. Once boiling, remove from heat immediately, strain, and serve in mugs.

Makes **8 servings.**

Variation:

- *Hot Apple Cider:* 5 cups apple juice, 2 pieces broken cinnamon bark and 2 cloves. In a large pot on high heat, combine all ingredients. Bring to a boil, then reduce heat and simmer for 10-15 minutes. Strain before serving.

Appendices

Seasons of the Year

JUST AS FOOD AFFECTS each *dosha*, so does each season. For example, winter and early spring have Kapha qualities that are cool, moist, and dormant, so every body type should compensate with more warming Pitta-increasing foods. The Pitta season, late spring and summer, gives Pittas a 'double dose' of fire. All body types should follow more cooling recipes and practices during this time, especially Pittas. The Vata season, autumn and early winter, tends to be full of movement. During this time, all *doshas* should be mindful of being grounded and follow a diet that will decrease Vata.

The Kapha season is winter and early spring. Balance by including extra outdoor activities in your regular exercise routine and increasing the amount of hot spices in your meals. Eat warm, light foods such as vegetable soups, as well as foods that are more pungent, bitter, and astringent. You should also decorate your surroundings with warm, vibrant colours.

The Pitta season is late spring and summer, when the heat is on. Balance by eating lighter, cooling, less spicy foods, as well as more fruits and salads. Decorate your surroundings with cool, soothing colours. Also try to rest and relax as much as possible near water or in the shade when it is hot.

The Vata season is autumn and early winter. This is a time to eat warmer, grounding foods, like cooked root vegetables and comfort foods like *Beat the Cold Soup* (page 98). Rest and restrict yourself to relaxing activities when possible; sit by a warm fire, or take a walk. Decorate your surroundings with earth tones to ground your energy.

Cleanses

Why should I do a cleanse? There are many types of cleanses that restore the body by eliminating toxins, thereby improving our ability to absorb nutrients. After cleansing, people usually find that their digestion improves, resulting in clear skin, more energy, and a healthier weight. Additionally, cleanses can balance moods and improve mental clarity, making you feel clear-headed and present. It is advisable to do a cleanse one to four times a year. Always consult a health professional or doctor before commencing any cleanse.

General tips: Be creative when preparing a cleansing menu. Experiment with various tea recipes. Discover the variety of fruits and vegetables available in your local markets. Make your salads colourful and adventurous; for example, add beets, carrots, avocados, nuts, watercress, dandelion greens, sprouts, onions, and/or nuts. Prepare tasty, invigorating dressings using lemon juice and cold-pressed oils (e.g., olive, flax seed, hemp, or sesame oils). Add garlic, ginger, salt, herbs, raisins, dried cranberries, and pomegranate, which impart great contrasting flavours. Always try to incorporate the Six Essential Tastes of Ayurveda: salty, sweet, sour, astringent, pungent, and bitter (page 21). Lastly, have fun with the choices you make!

TWELVE-DAY CLEANSE

Start the Twelve-Day Cleanse on a Monday so that Days 6 and 7 (when only liquids are consumed) fall on a Saturday and Sunday. Alternatively, if you find you get hungrier on weekends and/or eat less while you are working, ensure that Days 6 and 7 fall on light workdays.

Start each day with a cup of hot lemon tea (juice of ½ a lemon in hot water; you may add a little fresh ginger and/or a pinch of cayenne). Try not to eat before 10 am. Avoid caffeine and alcohol and other stimulants during this purifying time — instead of coffee, drink herbal tea or purified water. If you find you are having major hunger pangs, drink a glass of water mixed with hemp protein powder.

Day 1: Eliminate eggs, seafood, chicken, and meat from diet.

Day 2: Eliminate dairy products.

Day 3: Eliminate grains, starches, and sugar.

Day 4: Eat only raw fruits, raw vegetables, and raw nuts.

Day 5: Same as Day 4.

Day 6: Liquids only (if the liquid-only-days are too challenging, you may substitute Days 6 and 7 with Day 4). Every two hours, drink(180-240 ml of warm water with lemon; you may add ginger, cayenne pepper, and turmeric. You may also drink lots of distilled or purified water, Parsley Tea (page 194) or Sage tea throughout the day. If your energy feels low, rest — let your body do its work and eliminate its toxins.

Day 7: Same as Day 6.

Day 8: Eat as much fresh fruit as you like, and drink as much water and herbal tea as you need.

Day 9: Eat raw fruits and raw vegetables; drizzle veggies with oil and lemon juice. Drink veggie juices, water, and herbal tea.

Day 10: Reincorporate grains, starches, and cooked vegetables.

Day 11: Reincorporate dairy.

Day 12: Same as Day 11.

Day 13: Reincorporate eggs, seafood, chicken, and meat.

WINTER CLEANSE

This is a variation of the Twelve-Day Cleanse, but with more warming foods for cooler winter days. Follow the same guidelines as in the introduction to the Twelve-Day Cleanse (page 202), including starting each day with hot lemon tea.

Day 1: Eliminate eggs, seafood, chicken, and meat from diet.
Day 2: Eliminate dairy products.
Day 3: Eliminate starches and sugar.
Day 4: Eliminate grains. Eat cooked soups and vegetable stews.
Day 5: Same as Day 4.
Day 6: Clear liquids only: e.g., *Clear Vegetable Soup* (page 94), Vata-calming teas and *Parsley Tea* (page 194) (If the liquid-only days are too challenging, you may substitute Days 6 and 7 with Day 4.).
Day 7: Same as Day 6.
Day 8: Reincorporate cooked vegetables such as in soups and stews.
Day 9: Same as Day 8.
Day 10: Reincorporate grains and starches.
Day 11: Reincorporate dairy.
Day 12: Reincorporate eggs, seafood, chicken, and meat (if not vegetarian).

Yoga Poses for the *Doshas*

YOGA IS AN INTEGRAL part of Ayurveda and the holistic healing process. Yoga, which means union, helps to connect mind, body, and spirit. By practicing yoga regularly, you will notice an increase in flexibility, your movements will be more graceful, and you will feel more grounded and in the present moment. If you are a beginner, be gentle on yourself and only go slightly past the point where you feel your muscles stretching. Do not strain yourself; pay attention to your body and allow your flexibility to slowly improve over time. Avoid self-judgment and let your mind clear as the various postures replenish and relax you. It may also be helpful to try beginner yoga classes and/or watch instructional yoga DVDs, particularly to get a better understanding of body alignment principles and modifications for poses. For your own daily personal practice, start with 5-10 minute sessions; over time, you will notice an increase in your ability, endurance, and energy levels.

It is important to begin each yoga session by lying down or sitting comfortably and focusing on your breathing. As you become aware of your inhales and exhales, also become aware of your body, mind, and emotions. Replenish yourself with long inhales. When you exhale, try to release more oxygen than you think you have inhaled, and notice the length and depth of your inhales expand. Visualize what parts of your body your breath reaches, dissolving any areas that feel tight or obstructed.

Specific breathing exercises can benefit specific *doshas*. Breathing to and from the abdomen helps to ground Vata. Breathing in and out from the ribcage, will give you a sense of empowerment, and is especially beneficial for Pitta. 'Complete breaths,' as does *The Fire Breath* (page 217), energize and enliven the entire body, especially for Kapha. For complete breaths, inhale to the lower abdomen and lower back first, then allow it to work its way up, filling the rib cage, then the mid- and upper-back, up to the collarbones and neck; your body should feel completely full of oxygen. Exhale slowly, allowing it to release from the upper body first, then the rib cage, followed by the mid- and lower back, and lastly the abdomen.

Breathing is a wonderful tool to bring us back into our bodies and nourish us at any time throughout the day. Take notice of how your breathing patterns may shift during the day and in what situations. According to Ayurvedic and yogic traditions, having control of (or being aware of) your breathing is the same thing as having control of your life. Use exhales to release old toxins, old beliefs, old attachments — anything that is not from the present moment — and use inhales to replenish every cell of your body with oxygen and light.

While practicing *asanas* continue to be aware of your body, and take note of where and how your breath travels through you. This will deepen your yoga practice and make it far more beneficial than if you only concentrate on alignment, strength, and flexibility.

Just as it is important to begin a yoga session with breath awareness, make sure you end each session in *savasana* (page 214) for 5-10 minutes. *Savasana* is an important cooling-down period when the body, mind, and spirit can integrate the benefits of the yoga session. You may also choose to do this in a *Seated Meditation pose* (page 216).

By following these suggestions, your body, mind, and spirit will, over time, radiate with light. Of course there will be ups and downs, but remember that the downs are crucial periods to continue practicing yoga as these are usually the times when we are transitioning from the past to a new period in life. It takes courage to practice yoga — by doing so, you are opening up your heart, body, and mind, becoming a fully functioning human being in the truest sense.

Sun Salutation is a beneficial way to begin the day for all *doshas*.

The Sun Salutation gives Kapha a wonderful kick-start to the day as this is a dynamic set of poses. Take one inhale and exhale in each posture to get Kapha moving. Complete 6-10 repetitions of the series.

To reduce and calm excess Vata, take 3 long inhales and exhales in each pose while focusing on alignment, not perfection. Complete 4-6 repetitions of the series.

Sun Salutations are also a good way for Pitta to become calm and centered for the day. To reduce Pitta, take 1-2 inhales and exhales in each pose to expel excess fire and increase inner focus while building natural strength. Complete 6-10 repetitions of the series.

Sun Salutation

Standing Mountain: Stand tall, letting your shoulders drop and spine lift as you root downward, evenly distributing your weight through the legs and feet. Place your hands together in prayer position, and notice how this helps to balance the right and left sides of your body and brain. On an inhale, raise the arms overhead. On an exhale, bend forward with a straight back into the Forward Bend.

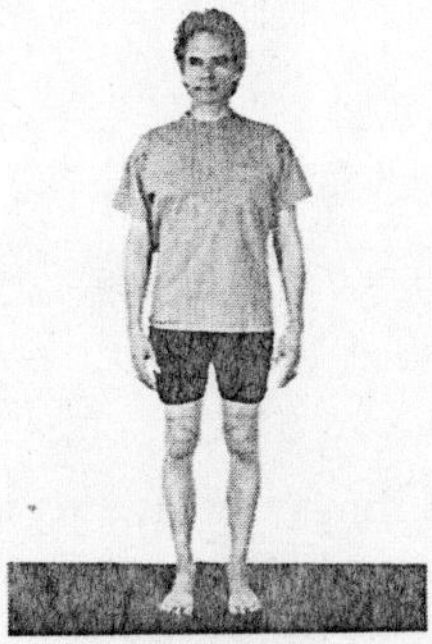
Standing Mountain

Forward Bend: The secret to this pose is letting the weight of your head surrender to gravity. As you hang your head down, imagine the spaces between each vertebra increasing. On the exhale, imagine toxins, old beliefs, and old attachments flowing down the spine and releasing through the top of the head. Inhale up the spine and widen the sacrum. Step back with your right foot to transition to the Lunge.

Forward Bend

Lunge: Feel your groin stretch, and lift your upper body out of the hip sockets. On the inhale, let your rib cage and heart expand in all directions. Step back with your left foot to transition to the Plank.

Plank: Ensure your hands are directly beneath the shoulders and use your arm strength. The insides of the elbows should face one another; avoid hyper-extending the elbows. Engage the abs and hips to protect the lower back (keep the hips from sagging) and inhale down to the heels. Transition down into Chataranga.

Lunge

Plank

Chataranga

Chataranga: From Plank, keep the elbows next to the sides of the body and the abs strong; lower the knees, chest, and chin towards the floor. Build the strength in your arms and abs by keeping the chest and chin just above the floor before transitioning to Cobra. (You can place a folded blanket for support).

Cobra: From Chataranga, let the chest be pulled forward and off the floor. Untuck the toes while engaging the lower back muscles and abs to protect the back. Keeping the elbows at the sides of your body, press the shoulder blades down, and let the inhale and exhale travel from the chest all the way down the torso and back out again. Press the upper quads to the floor. Relax the neck and face as you lean back. Transition to Downward Dog by curling the toes under and pushing the sitting bones up and back.

Downward Dog: Press down through the palms of your hands, lengthening the arms and the spine as you point the sitting bones up and back. Stretch the calves and backs of the legs as the heels press toward the floor. Keep the abs engaged to support the back as it widens and lengthens in Downward Dog. Step forward with the right foot for Reverse Lunge.

Downward Dog

Reverse Lunge

Reverse Lunge: For this second lunge in the series, always ensure that the opposite leg from the first lunge is forward so you strengthen both sides of the body. Focus on lengthening through the back leg and stretching through the bent hip. Stay supported with the abs and breathe. Next, step forward with the back foot to Forward Bend (page 207), then transition to the Supported Forward Bend.

Supported Forward Bend: From Forward Bend, straighten back, and lift up through the abs, coming up halfway out of the fold. Let the fingers rest on the floor or shins. Stay strong through the quads, allowing the backs of the legs to stretch. Keep the collarbones long, the chest open, and the head in line with the spine. With a straight back, return to Standing Mountain (page 207) to complete the Sun Salutation.

Repeat the series according to your *dosha* (page 17), ensuring that you alternate which foot steps back for the first Lunge.

Supported Forward Bend

KAPHA POSES

Counteracting Kapha's slow-moving state requires stimulating, heat-building exercises that utilize Kapha's gift of stamina. Kaphas should take short rests between each asana, vary your yoga routine, and go slightly beyond your limit. These are especially good for a Kapha body type; however, all poses (including those for Vata and Pitta) are beneficial for Kapha, especially if they are done in an invigorating way.

Forward Bend (page 207) is useful for reducing Kapha as it stimulates and tones the digestive system.

Cobra (page 208) stretches the abdomen and relieves constipation.

Downward Dog warms while building strength and flexibility. Practice breathing awareness through the entire body to energize Kapha. (**Variation — Walk the Dog:** bend alternate legs as you stretch the calves, or alternately raise each leg while maintaining support and alignment through grounding arms and leg.)

Bridge regulates the thyroid gland to balance metabolic rates, especially beneficial to Kapha. Lie on your back, bend the knees, and place the feet hip-width apart and parallel. Press the hips into the air and use the strength in the legs and buttocks to hold you up, pushing the hips higher while sending energy down to the feet. Press the shoulder blades toward each other and away from the neck and clasp the hands. To release the pose, slowly lower the spine.

Shoulder Stand brings blood to the thyroid gland, helping to reduce Kapha by stimulating and balancing the metabolism. If you are a beginner, lie on a folded blanket and place your legs up a wall. Over time, work your way into full Shoulder Stand by lifting the hips from the floor and supporting your back by keeping the abs engaged and hands behind

Shoulder Stand

the lower back. Lift one leg at a time away from the wall. Keep elbows shoulder-width apart and ensure your head can easily move from side to side. (Note: avoid inverted poses — when head is below the heart — while menstruating.)

From Shoulder Stand, transition to Plough: keeping the back supported with engaged abs and hands at the lower back, bring the knees towards the ears and extend the legs out over your head, aiming the toes for the floor behind you. To come out of the pose, use the strength of the abs to gently uncurl, slowly lowering the spine, then the legs to the floor. Follow with Fish pose.

Fish increases circulation to the spine and brain and calms the mind, and is a good counter pose to Shoulder Stand. Lay flat on your back. Place the hands behind the back and then press them against the hips. Using your elbows for support, lift your upper body off the floor. Allow your neck and head to release back toward the floor. Let the chest, upper and mid-back widen as you inhale, allowing the shoulders to broaden. Follow with Bridge (page 210).

Advanced Fish: For a deeper backward bend, place the wrists under your sitting bones (beneficial for relieving carpal tunnel syndrome), lift your upper body off the floor, and tilt the head back until it touches the floor. Inhale into the chest.

Sitting Twist tones the abdominal muscles while stimulating metabolism and digestive fire, and helps to detoxify while increasing energy and flexibility. Sit tall and bend your left leg under the right knee. Stretch up the left arm and turn to the right, placing the left elbow outside of the right knee. Place the right hand on the floor at the tailbone. Press the sitting bones into the ground and gently twist to the right, gazing over your right shoulder. On each exhale, twist a little more. Repeat on the other side.

Sitting Twist

PITTA POSES

People who are born with predominantly Pitta characteristics generally have stamina, vitality, and muscular bodies, allowing them to engage in intense yoga sessions as long as they do cooling postures, like a Forward Bend (page 207) or Savasana (page 214), at the end. To reduce Pitta, perform these poses in a calm, relaxed fashion while staying aware of the connections to mind, body, and spirit. These poses are good for reducing Pitta; however, all the poses are beneficial if they are done with a relaxed yet alert mind.

Side Triangle

Side Triangle is an excellent pose for lengthening and strengthening the sides of the body. Start standing with feet one leg-length apart, with weight evenly distributed on both feet. Stretch the arms out, parallel to the floor, on either side of you. Turn the left foot out, reach the left arm out to the left, and then stretch the left fingers down to the floor on the inside of the left foot. If your fingers cannot touch the floor, rest them on a block. Ensure you do not feel compression on the left side of the body. Work towards looking up at your right thumb while maintaining strength and stretching through the legs and sides of the body. Focus on your breathing, imagine it opening the rib cage as you open the chest, twist the spine, and lengthen the arms and legs. Repeat on other side.

Dancer requires balance and concentration. Standing on the left leg, take your right foot in your right hand and bend it back to the right buttock, allowing the right quadriceps to stretch. Once you have mastered standing on one leg, gradually extend your left arm above your head. To extend deeper in Dancer pose, press the right foot continually into the right hand, allowing the spine to curve, and reach forward through the left hand. Repeat on the other side.

Pigeon opens the front of the body and balances the digestive fire, especially useful for Pitta. Start on your hands and knees. Bend the right knee forward to place it under the chest, then extend the left leg back. With hands on either side of you for balance, lift the chest, allowing the weight of the body to stretch and open the hips. Repeat on other side.

Advanced Pigeon: Lean forward and rest your head on your fists or on the floor. Breathe deeply, allowing thoughts to slow down while the hips open. Repeat on other side, or walk hands back to starting Pigeon position with the chest lifted. Bend the left leg and reach the left hand back to hold the left foot. Gently pull the left foot toward the left sitting bone, stretching the quadriceps and groin while continually raising the upper body and opening the chest. Repeat on other side.

Bow massages the abdominal organs. Lie with your stomach down on a mat. Bend the knees, and take hold of the feet at the outsides. Pull the feet towards the sitting bones while pressing the feet back into the hands. Allow the shoulders to roll back and the head and chest to lift off the mat. Breathe as you relax the neck and face.

Reclining Bound-Angle lifts the diaphragm away from the stomach and liver, helping to relieve acid reflux and revitalize digestive organs. Ensure you are comfortable and able to fully relax in order to maximize the benefits of this pose. Lie back on a bolster (or a rolled-up blanket) placed along the spine from the neck to the waist or sacrum. Press the outsides of the soles of your feet together and allow the knees to open and fall to each side.

Bow

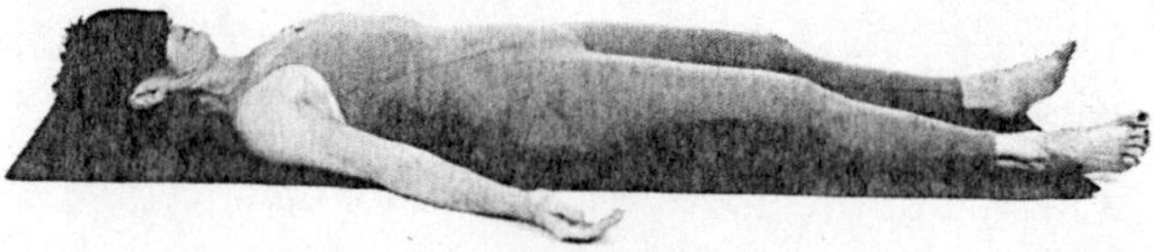

Savasana

Savasana diffuses excess heat and relaxes the abdomen. Lie flat on your back (or on a bolster, see Reclining Bound-Angle) with feet side by side and arms at your side with the palms of your hands facing up. Close your eyes and release your entire body, imagining it melting into the floor. Take long, calm breaths, drawing the inhales down to fill the belly, imagining the space your yoga practice has created in your body being filled with radiant light. Remain in savasana for 5-10 minutes.

VATA POSES

Slower meditative yoga that focuses on the breath is best for calming Vata. Standing poses which require concentration and focus quiet the typically active Vata mind. Hold each pose for 3-6 breaths, focusing on alignment and opening the body to breath. Concentrate on building stability and staying grounded. The Wind-Relieving poses and Forward Bend also help to balance Vata. These poses are especially useful for a Vata body type, however, all yoga poses are beneficial when done slowly and steadily. Make sure to end your yoga session with a long savasana and meditation.

Wind-Relieving Pose: Lie on your back. With the left leg stretched out, pull the right knee in towards you, gently stretching the right quad and groin. Try to press your nose to the right knee to stretch the neck and use the abdominal muscles to support the back. Repeat with the other leg.

Cat: On your hands and knees, as you inhale, lift the head as you look up, and allow the spine to drop. As you exhale, drop the head, tuck the chin toward the chest, and arch the spine like an angry cat, pulling in the abdominal cavity. Repeat 4-6 times. Keep the movements connected to your inhales and exhales as you focus on opening the vertebrae of the spine, releasing Kundalini energy.

Side Twist is a balancing pose requiring concentration and focus, relieving the Vata wind and quieting the Vata's busy mind. While squatting with the knees together, twist your body to the right, drawing the left elbow over the right thigh. Press the palms of your hands together and look up towards your right elbow. Repeat on other side.

Forward Bend (page 207): Focus on lengthening the spine and bringing the head towards the knees, releasing old energy through the crown of the head.

Butterfly

Butterfly opens the first chakra (energy center in the body) at the tailbone, which reduces anxiety, an attribute of Vata. Sit with a tall spine, imagining a golden cord gently pulling the crown of your head upward. Hold the outsides of your feet and press the soles together. Press the knees towards the floor. Allow the inner thighs to stretch, and over time your hips and knees will release more and more.

TRIDOSHIC POSE

This is a great pose for all *doshas* to practice at the end of a yoga session.

Seated Meditation: Yoga leads the way to meditation, as the poses open our bodies and quiet our minds, clearing way for connecting with our spirit — the ultimate goal of yoga. Sit with a tall spine and sacrum wide. Close your eyes. Imagine your body filling with light through the top of the head, down the spine, and through every cell. (I call this filling up at a free cosmic gas station!) Maintain pose for 2-5 minutes or longer.

Seated Meditation

Alternate Ayurvedic Therapies

THIS SECTION INCLUDES AYURVEDIC activities such as breathing techniques, aromatherapy and colour therapy, a five-minute massage, and visualization that will help you to maintain a stress-free, healthy, and joyful lifestyle.

PRANAYAMA: BREATHING TECHNIQUES

Pra means 'to live,' or 'to breathe'; *pranayama*, is the practice of yogic breathing. Pranayama techniques feed, stimulate, and regulate the vital life force in our bodies. As we say in yoga, when you have control over your breath, you have control over your life. *Pranayama* refers to the practice of breath awareness ('I am breathing in, I am breathing out'), which expands our capacity to breathe. It is also a method of clearing both the body and the mind in order to reveal our true nature. Breath awareness supplies our blood, organs, and brains with vital oxygen, which helps to increase mental clarity and our power of concentration. Below are two pranayama techniques:

The Fire Breath

Some people pay to go to oxygen chambers when there is a simple way to get the same benefits for free! This is an energizing breathing exercise that increases the 'pure life force,' sometimes called *chi* or *kundalini*. It is excellent for reducing Kapha, as it stimulates energy and diminishes feelings of lethargy.

Sit in a comfortable position with your spine straight, imagining the spaces between your vertebrae opening. Concentrate on breathing in and out from your abdomen. Inhale deeply through your nostrils into your abdomen, then pull your abdomen inward — aiming the belly button back to the spine — for a quick exhale through the nostrils. Repeat this 20 times, then take a break, letting the increased oxygen permeate your entire body. Repeat until you do 5 sets of 20. Over time, you can work towards doing this 100 times without a break.

Alternate Nostril Breathing

This breathing exercise is good for all *doshas* and balances the right and left sides of the body. We often have a dominant side of the brain, either the right brain (considered the female or yin side) or the left brain (considered the male or yang side). Alternate nostril breathing helps to then regulate, clear, and balance us, making ourselves much more capable and creative in addressing situations in our lives.

Try this breathing technique if you are having trouble sleeping at night or at any time you want to feel clear, centered, and balanced.

Begin by taking the index finger of the left hand, blocking your right nostril, and inhaling through the left nostril (if you wish to use your right hand simply switch to place the index finger on the left nostril and the thumb on the right). Now block the left nostril with your thumb as you exhale through the right. Inhale through the right nostril then block the right nostril as you exhale through the left. Keep alternating, but do not continue for more than 5 minutes. If you feel light-headed, concentrate on breathing into your low belly.

AROMATHERAPY

Aromatherapy is the application or inhalation of essential oils to positively affect one's mood or health. Many essential oils have medicinal properties than can calm and heal, and in Ayurveda, they balance and calm the *doshas*. Allow your own sense of smell to determine which essential oils your body responds to at different times of the day or year; don't be afraid to work intuitively.

Vata can be balanced with orange, rose, geranium, lavender, cinnamon, clove, and sandalwood as well as other warm, sweet, or sour essential oils.

Pitta can be balanced with mint, lavender, rose, jasmine, clary sage, lemon, and lemongrass as well as other cool or sweet essential oils.

Kapha can be balanced with eucalyptus, mint, clove, marjoram, camphor, juniper, lemon, orange, basil, bergamot, and sage as well as other uplifting essential oils.

A few drops of any essential oil can be added to water, burned in an essential oil burner, or sprinkled in a room. Add 10 drops of any essential oil to 20 ml of any carrier oil to use for a massage or add to a warm bath.

In addition, orange peels and cloves can be simmered on a stove to balance Vata and Kapha. Lavender can be sprinkled on a pillow or placed in a bowl (fresh or dry) to balance both Vata and Pitta. Shells or rocks can be sprinkled with any oil and left in a room; these can be refreshed from time to time.

Carrier oils are generally cold-pressed vegetable oils that are used to dilute essential oils for aromatherapy, massages, or baths, and also can be used on their own to soothe your dosha: to reduce Vata, use sesame, castor, or flaxseed oil; to reduce Pitta, use coconut or olive oil; to reduce Kapha, use sweet almond or safflower oil. These oils should always be cold-pressed to retain their vitamins.

COLOUR THERAPY

Using the colours of the light spectrum to stimulate the body's own healing process, colour therapy balances energy wherever our bodies may be lacking, be it physically, emotionally, spiritually, or mentally. With Ayurveda, you can use different colours according to your *dosha*.

If you are new to colour therapy, have fun experimenting with how colours affect your moods and energy levels. Notice how different colours in nature make you feel: compare gazing on a bright blue ocean to a deep orange sunset; or a dark starry sky or a somber grey morning to a dark green forest. Looking at differently coloured paint chips can be another effective way to become more conscious of how colour affects you. Once attuned, you can increase your energy, serenity, and sense of well-being as a result of colour choices in your clothing, home, or workplace.

Vata can be balanced with white, green, violet, magenta, turquoise, and red.

Pitta can be balanced with white, green, deep ocean blue, violet, magenta, pale pinks, and turquoise. (Avoid strong colours such as red and black.)

Kapha can be balanced with red, orange, and magenta. Turquoise and green are also beneficial.

Here is a list of some colours and their properties:

- **Blue** cools, soothes, and increases clarity. It calms Vata and Pitta and lifts Kapha.
- **Green** calms, refreshes, and gives a feeling of being in nature. It harmonizes all *doshas* and is valued for healing medical conditions such as tumors.
- **Magenta** helps us to let go of obsessive attachments and the past, and promotes happiness. It is balancing for all *doshas*.

- **Orange** is energizing and joyous, increases sexual energy, and strengthens the immune system. It is uplifting for Kapha.
- **Red** is fiery, passionate, and powerful. It is assertive, courageous, and vital. It aids willpower. It warms Vata, energizes Kapha, and increases Pitta.
- **Turquoise** is cool, refreshing, and energizing, and is also an anti-inflammatory. It helps get rid of stagnation and reduces fevers. It can be used as a protection from unwanted energies. It benefits all the *doshas*.
- **Violet** promotes insight, intuition, and self-love. It is especially beneficial for Vata and Pitta.

FIVE-MINUTE ABHYANGA MASSAGE

This invigorating Ayurvedic massage strengthens your immune system and increases circulation, leaving you feeling refreshed. This massage takes only a few minutes and can be done anywhere, just ensure it is done at least half an hour before eating. If you have more time, you may add oil to this massage: sesame or almond oil for Vata; cold-pressed olive, coconut, or sunflower oil for Pitta; or corn, mustard, safflower, or almond oil for Kapha.

Start by standing or sitting. Briskly rub the palms of your hands together for 10-20 seconds. Place your left hand over your left ear and right hand over your right ear, then briskly run your hands back and forth over your ears for 10-20 seconds; this touches all the acupressure points, or *nadis*, on the ears that invigorate the entire body. Next, use both palms to lightly wipe or clean the aura around your head using downward movements. Shake your hands as one would flick water off to clear energy. Next, run your palms down the front and back of your body with downward strokes, using circular motions for all major joints (e.g., shoulders, elbows, knees); keep shaking the hands to get rid of old energy.

GROUNDING VISUALIZATION

This tridoshic grounding method will leave you feeling rooted and confident of your true self, rather than feeling under the influence of or bogged down by the world around you.

Stand with your feet parallel and close together with your weight evenly distributed. Push your feet firmly to the ground and imagine you are pulling up the energy of the earth through your feet. Keeping the leg muscles engaged, without locking the knees, stand tall. Let your tailbone drop and tuck under while pulling your belly button inwards to the spine, and feeling a lift in the pubic bone. Feel your upper body lift out of your hipbones, and the spine lengthening upwards, imagining the spaces between your vertebrae widen. Let your shoulders drop down. Continue the upward-lengthening of the spine: imagine the neck vertebrae lengthening upward and widening the base of your skull, then imagine the brain fluids that reside here flowing easily. Visualize any stiffness in the neck dissolving, allowing a clear passage for energy to flow between the mind and body.

Now, with this full body-awareness, imagine pulling in energy from the sun above, like a golden light, through the top of your head, running down through the spine and through the bones of your legs, rooting you deeply to the earth.

With practice, you will be able to do this visualization in a few seconds wherever you are, grounding yourself in who you are while centering yourself in the present moment.

Food Guidelines for Basic Constitutional Types*

FRUITS

Vata		Pitta		Kapha	
AVOID	TAKE	AVOID	TAKE	AVOID	TAKE
Dried Fruits	Apricots	Apples, sour	Apples, sweet	Avocado	Apples
Apples	Avocado	Apricots, sour	Apricots, sweet	Bananas	Apricots
Cranberries	Bananas	Berries, sour	Avocado	Coconut	Berries
Pears	All berries	Bananas	Berries, sweet	Dates	Cherries
Pomegranat	Cherries	Cherries, sour	Coconut	Figs, fresh	Cranberries
Prunes	Coconut	Cranberries	Dates	Grapefruit	Figs, dry
Watermelon	Dates	Grapefruit	Figs	Lemons	Mango
	Figs, fresh	Grapes, green	Grapes, sweet	Limes	Peaches
	Grapefruit	Lemons	Mango	Melons	Pears
	Melons	Limes, in excess	Melons	Oranges	Pomegranate
	Oranges	Papaya	Oranges, sweet	Papaya	Prunes
	Papaya	Peaches	Pears	Pineapples	Raisins
	Peaches	Pineapples, sour	Pineapples, sweet	Plums	**Moderation**
	Pineapples	Plums, sour	Plums, sweet	Rhubarb	Strawberries
	Plums	Rhubarb	Pomegranate	Watermelon	
	Raisins, soaked	Strawberries	Prunes	**Moderation**	
	Rhubarb	**Moderation**	Raisins	Grapes	
	Strawberries	Kiwi	Watermelon	Kiwi	

*Reprinted with permission from *The Ayurvedic Cookbook* by Amadea Morningstar with Urmila Desai (Lotus Press, 1990).

**Fruit and fruit juices are best consumed by themselves for all *doshas*.

GRAINS

Vata AVOID	Vata TAKE	Pitta AVOID	Pitta TAKE	Kapha AVOID	Kapha TAKE
Cold, dry, puffed cereals Buckwheat Corn Granola Millet Oat bran Oats, dry Rye Wheat bran (in excess) **Occasionally** Barley Rice cakes	Oats, cooked All Rice, including brown rice Wheat Wild rice **Moderation** Amaranth	Buckwheat Corn Millet Oat granola Oats, dry Rye **Moderation** Oat bran **Occasionally** Amaranth Rice, brown	Barley Oats, cooked Rice, basmati or white Rice cakes Wheat Wheat bran Wheat granola	Oats, cooked Rice, brown or white Wheat	Barley Buckwheat Corn Granola, low-fat Millet Oat bran Oats, dry Rice, basmati, small amount with clove or peppercorn Rye **Moderation** Amaranth **Occasionally** Rice, cakes Wheat bran

SEEDS

Vata AVOID	Vata TAKE	Pitta AVOID	Pitta TAKE	Kapha AVOID	Kapha TAKE
Occasionally Psyllium	Flax Sesame Pumpkin Sunflower	Flax Sesame	Psyllium Sunflower **Moderation** Pumpkin	Psyllium Sesame	**Moderation** Flax Pumpkin Sunflower

VEGETABLES

Frozen, raw or dried vegetables Bell peppers Brussels sprouts Cabbage Cauliflower Celery Eggplant Mushrooms Onions, raw Peas Potatoes Tomatoes Turnips **Moderation** Beet greens Lettuce Parsley Spinach Sprouts Turnip green **Occasionally** Broccoli Corn, fresh	Artichoke Asparagus Beets Carrots Cucumber Green beans well-cooked Leeks, cooked Mustard greens Okra,cooked Olives black & green Onions, cooked Parsnip Potato,sweet Pumpkin Radish Watercress Zucchini **Moderation** Fenugreek	Beets Beet greens Fenugreek Garlic Mustard greens Olives green Onions, raw Radish Tomatoes Turnip greens Turnips **Moderation** Onions, cooked **Occasionally** Carrots Eggplant Kohlrabi Leeks, cooked Pumpkin Spinach	Artichokes Asparagus Bell peppers Broccoli Brussels sprouts Cabbage Corn, fresh Cauliflower Cucumber Celery Green beans Lettuce Mushrooms Okra Parsley Parsnip Peas Sweet Potatoes Sprouts Zucchini **Moderation** Olives black Watercress	Sweet & juicy vegetables Cucumber Olives, black or green Potatoes, sweet Pumpkin Tomatoes Zucchini **Moderation** Artichokes **Occasionally** Parsnip	Raw vegetables Asparagus Bell peppers Broccoli Brussel sprouts Cabbage Carrots Cauliflower Celery Corn (fresh) Eggplant Fenugreek Garlic Green beans Lettuce Mushrooms Okra Onions Parsley Peas Potatoes (white) Radish Spinach Sprouts Turnip greens

LEGUMES

Vata		Pitta		Kapha	
AVOID	TAKE	AVOID	TAKE	AVOID	TAKE
Black beans	Urad dal	Urad dal	Aduki beans	Urad dal	Aduki beans
Black-eyed peas	**Moderation**	Masoor dal	Black beans	Brown or green lentils	Black beans
Brown or green lentils	Mung beans	Tur dal	Black-eyed peas	Kidney beans	Black-eyed peas
Chana dal	Masoor dal		Brown or green lentils	Soy beans	Chana dal
Chickpeas	Soy cheese		Chana dal	Soy milk, cold	Chickpeas
Kidney beans	Soy milk, liquid		Chickpeas	Soy cheese	Lima beans
Lima beans	Tofu		Kala chana	Soy flour	Kala chana
Soy beans	Tur dal		Kidney beans	Soy powder	lentils
Soy flour			Lima beans	Tofu, cold	Split peas
Soy powder			Mung beans	**Moderation**	Tur dal
Split peas			Soy beans	Mung beans	White beans
White beans			Soy cheese		**Moderation**
Moderation			Soy milk, liquid		Soy milk, hot
Kala chana			Split peas		Tofu, hot
			Tofu		
			White beans		
			Moderation		
			Soy flour		
			Soy powder		

NUTS					
	Walnuts **Moderation** Almonds Brazil nuts Cashews Coconut Hazelnuts Pecans Pine nuts Pistachios **Occasionally** Peanuts	Almonds Brazil nuts Cashews Hazelnuts Peanuts Pecans Pine Nuts Pistachios Walnuts		Almonds Brazil nuts Cashews Coconut Hazelnuts Peanuts Pecans Pine nuts Pistachios Walnuts	
DAIRY					
Goat's milk, powdered	**Moderation** All dairy	Butter, salted Buttermilk, commercial Cheese, hard or Feta Sour cream Yogurt	Butter, unsalted Cheese Ghee Ice cream Milk, cow's or goat's Yogurt, diluted, 1:2-3 pts water	Butter Cheese, all kinds Buttermilk, commercial Ice cream Milk, cow's Sour cream Yogurt, undiluted	Ghee Milk, goat's Yogurt, diluted, 1:4pts or more with water

SWEETENERS

Vata		Pitta		Kapha	
AVOID	TAKE	AVOID	TAKE	AVOID	TAKE
White sugar	Barley malt syrup Brown rice syrup Fructose Fruit juice concentrates Gur Honey Maple syrup Molasses Sugar cane juice	Gur Molasses **Moderation** Honey	Barley malt syrup Brown rice syrup Maple syrup Fruit juice concentrates Fructose Sugar cane juice **Moderation** White sugar	Barley malt syrup Brown rice syrup Fructose Gur Maple syrup, in excess Molasses Sugar cane juice White sugar	Raw honey Fruit juice concentrates, esp. apple and pear

OILS

Vata		Pitta		Kapha	
AVOID	TAKE	AVOID	TAKE	AVOID	TAKE
	All oils, esp. sesame	Almond Apricot Corn Safflower Sesame	**Moderation** Avocado Coconut Olive Sesame Sunflower Soy walnut	Apricot Avocado Coconut Olive Safflower Sesame Soy Walnut	In very small amounts: Almond Corn Sunflower

CONDIMENTS

Ketchup **Moderation** Chili peppers Ginger, dry **Occasionally** Onion, raw Sprouts	Black sesame seeds Coconut Cottage cheese Garlic Ghee Ginger, fresh Lemon Lime pickle Mango, chutney Mango, pickle Mayonnaise Mustard Onion, cooked Papaya chutney Radish Salt Seaweeds Sesame seeds Soy sauce Yogurt **Moderation** Black pepper Lettuce Mint leaves	Black sesame seeds Cheese, grated Chili peppers Garlic Ginger Ketchup Mustard Lemon Lime Lime pickle Mango pickle Mayonnaise Onions, esp. raw Papaya chutney Radish Salt, in excess Seaweed, unrinsed, in excess Sesame seeds Soy sauce Yogurt, undiluted	Coconut Cottage cheese Ghee Lettuce Mango chutney Mint leaves Sprouts **Moderation** Black pepper	Black sesame seeds Cheese, grated Coconut Ketchup Lemon Lime Lime pickle Mango chutney Mango pickles Mayonnaise Papaya chutney Salt Sesame seeds Soy sauce Yogurt **Moderation** Cottage cheese Seaweeds, well-rinsed	Black pepper Chili peppers Garlic Ginger, esp. dry Lettuce Mint leaves Mustard Onions Radish Sprouts **Moderation** Ghee

SPICES

Vata		Pitta		Kapha	
AVOID	TAKE	AVOID	TAKE	AVOID	TAKE
Moderation	Ajwain	Ajwain	Coriander	Amchoor	Ajwain
Neem leaves	Almond extract	Amchoor	Cumin	Tamarind	Asafoetida
	Amchoor	Asafoetida	Dill	**Moderation**	Basil
	Asafoetida	Basil	Fennel	Almond extract	Bay leaf
	Basil	Bay leaf	Mint		Black pepper
	Bay leaf	Cayenne	Neem leaves		Caraway
	Black pepper	Cloves	Peppermint		Cardamom
	Caraway	Fenugreek	Rose water		Cayenne
	Cardamom	Garlic, esp. raw	Saffron		Cinnamon
	Cinnamon	Ginger	Spearmint		Cloves
	Cloves	Mace	Turmeric		Coriander
	Coriander	Marjoram	Wintergreen		Cumin
	Cumin	Mustard seeds	**Moderation**		Dill
	Dill	Nutmeg	Basil leaves, fresh		Fenugreek
	Fennel	Onion, esp. raw	Black pepper		Garlic
	Garlic	Oregano	Cardamom		Ginger, esp. dry
	Ginger	Paprika	Cinnamon		Mace
	Marjoram	Pippali	Orange peel		Marjoram
	Mint	Rosemary	Parsley		Mint
	Mustard seeds	Sage	Vanilla		Mustard seeds
	Nutmeg	Savory			Neem leaves
	Onion, cooked	Tarmarind			Nutmeg
	Orange peel	Thyme			Onion

SPICES *continued*

	Oregano Paprika Parsley Peppermint Poppy seeds Rosemary Rose water Saffron Sage Spearmint Tamarind Thyme Turmeric **Moderation** Cayenne Fenugreek	**Moderation** Almond extract Caraway Poppy seeds			Orange peel Oregano Paprika Parsley Peppermint Poppy seeds Rosemary Rose water Saffron Sage Spearmint Thyme Turmeric **Moderation** Fennel

SEEDS

Occasionally Psyllium	Flax Sesame Pumpkin Sunflower	Flax Sesame	Psyllium Sunflower **Moderation** Pumpkin	Psyllium Sesame	**Moderation** Flax Pumpkin Sunflower

Also available

Ayurvedic Cure for Common Diseases

Dr. N. A. Murthy and D. P. Pandey

The book shares the millenia of Ayurvedic experience of preventing and effectively treating over 100 common and not-so-common ailments, using time proven concepts of regulated diet and a healthy lifestyle, supported with remedies and treatments that are safe, effective and affordable.

'...provides information on home remedies for certain diseases alongwith standard Ayurvedic preparation.'

Hindu

Nature Cure for Common Diseases

Vithaldas Modi

Naturopathy or nature cure can successfully treat many common and chronic ailments, including some that other systems may not be able to. The methods are simple, safe, non-toxic, non-habit forming, without adverse effects.

'Comprehensive... presents in a simple straight-forward and convincing manner the advantages of natural cures in aiding recovery from all acute and chronic ailments and conditions and in maintaining health and vitality.'

The Hindustan Times

Available at all leading bookshops | Orient Publishing

www.orientpublishing.com